Rei

# Healing Through The
# ELEMENTS

## Ashwita Goel

**Copyright © 2018 by Ashwita Goel.**

**Published by** Reiki Rays: http://www.ReikiRays.com

All rights reserved. No part of this book may be reproduced by any mechanical, photographic or electronic process, or in the form of a phonographic recording; nor may it be stored in a retrieval system, transmitted or otherwise be copied for public or private use, other than for 'fair use' as brief quotations embodied in articles and reviews, without prior written permission of the publisher.

The author of this book does not dispense medical advice or prescribe the use of any technique as a form of treatment for physical or medical problems without the advice of a physician, either directly or indirectly. The intent of this website is only to offer information of a general nature to help you in your quest for emotional and spiritual well-being. In the event that you use any of the information in this book for yourself, which is your constitutional right, the author, this author and the publisher assume no responsibility for your actions.

For my Family

# Contents

PREFACE ..................................................... vii
INTRODUCTION ............................................. 1
AKASH (ETHER/ SPACE) ................................... 9
VAYU (AIR) ................................................. 19
TEJAS/ AGNI (FIRE) ....................................... 29
APAS (WATER) ............................................. 41
PRITHVI (EARTH) .......................................... 55
POWERFUL COMBINATIONS ........................... 67
PUTTING IT ALL TOGETHER ............................ 77
OTHER PHILOSOPHIES ................................... 85
FINDING BALANCE THROUGH FOOD ................ 89
MASSAGE & BODY SCRUBS ........................... 101
MUDRAS AND THE ELEMENTS ....................... 111
ELEMENTS AND LIVING SPACES ..................... 127
ELEMENTS AND THE ZODIAC ........................ 133
ESOTERIC TOOLS ........................................ 139

**THE IDEAL SPIRITUAL PATHWAY ..............................153**
**JOURNEYING THROUGH THE ELEMENTS ...............161**
**BIBLIOGRAPHY ................................................................165**
**ABOUT THE AUTHOR ....................................................169**
**ALSO BY ASHWITA GOEL ..............................................171**

# PREFACE

*Never separate the life you live from the words you speak.*
*~ Paul Wellstone*

I remember how as a child, I would sit on my terrace, feel the breeze and imagine that I *was* the breeze. Then there were nights when I'd meditate, allowing myself to expand and be the void sometimes, and at other times, imagining that fire was consuming my body; summer evenings spent lazing on the lawn, letting the body disappear into the earth, and occasional visits to the beach where I'd imagine I was the sea. For me they were just products of a wild imagination, things I was too embarrassed to share when my sister pestered me with a 'what do you do when you are meditating?!' It was many years before I realised what I had been doing.

It is quite amazing what we can do when we are just left to ourselves without interference from belief systems and people. So nothing in this book is really new, it is just a reminder of everything you have already known deep inside. If you have been on a spiritual pathway already, chances are high that you would have found a deepening of your connection with your body and that the body is already guiding you. The purpose of this book is to help make all that information conscious, so that you can also take conscious steps towards healing imbalances along with letting your body naturally steer you towards healing.

My own connection with the body and the elements was put to the test quite intensely while writing this book – something I had never expected. I didn't realise it at the start, when I started writing the chapter on ether. Within a day, I was done with the chapter and thought *'ok, I think I'm going to release a 15 page mini-book'*. Little did I know I was meditating on the void, and it was not that easy to come up with much substance!

As I started writing about air, I realised there was so much to write, but it was a nightmare trying to manage all my other commitments and my mind was completely full of stuff all the time!

Having had issues with personal power for many years, fire is a central theme of my life and obviously, I experienced nervousness for two whole days before I even started that chapter. I realised why after I started it. I had a huge meltdown, losing my temper and shouting at the top of my voice for something that shouldn't have become a fight in the first place. This is extremely unusual for me and left me terrified of who I had become. As my body burned in the winter, my breath burning and waking me up in the middle of the nights I would wonder, 'what have I gotten myself into?' But then I was starting to get the hang of it.

The water chapter almost instantly calmed the fire and then proceeded to take me to the other end. It had me PMSing and crying because I didn't get the lunch I had wanted. This is embarrassing even to remember! The earth was the hardest bit, since things would just not move – so typical of the 'resistance' that the earth represents. I would work on every other area of the book, and this is where the ether chapter got a whole lot more information as well, but the earth chapter itself just moved in jolts and with so little flow.

And I am so grateful to have gone through all of this. Apart from teaching me so much more than I already knew, it has enriched this book immensely as I brought to it everything I was using to come back from a state of extreme imbalance into normalcy.

By the time I was done writing this book, I had learned to give myself more space, my mind was much sharper, my eyes had been opened to so many things which were hidden from my awareness for months, I was able to take back the power I was giving away, able to love and nourish myself more deeply and be more present in my body than before.

When writing this book in itself has been such a deep, moving experience, I can only imagine what it might facilitate in the reader. Read it with an openness to heal, and you might find balance in your body, mind, emotions, relationships and profession through this journey – because nothing in the material world can exist without the five elements, and a deeper understanding can change everything.

# INTRODUCTION

*Nothing exists except atoms and empty space;
everything else is an opinion.*
~ *Democritus*

There are various perspectives to look at the world with. One can look at it as *advaita* – everything is one, or in terms of duality - yin and yang, energy and mass from the scientific perspective, or as the trinity – creator, sustainer, destroyer or as the five elements.

Chinese philosophy categorizes the five elements as earth, water, fire, metal and wood, while the Indian *Sānkhya* philosophy separates the world into earth, water, fire, air and ether. We can try to reach a state of balance through any of these methods, and here I share how we can get there by understanding the role of the *pancha* (five) *mahā* (great) *bhuta* (elements).

Ultimately, the secret to good health - physically, mentally, emotionally and otherwise, is balance. It is a narrow path to tread since little things can send us out of balance. Understanding life from the perspective of the 5 elements helps us restore this balance more easily.

For anyone on the spiritual pathway also, this understanding can be tremendously helpful. Looking at it from a Chakra point of view, the five elements rule the first 5 Chakras. It is only when these 5 Chakras are balanced and stable that one can truly open up to the power of the third eye and eventually the expansion of the Crown. Many of us have a tendency to get over zealous at some point or the other, overdo our *sadhana* and hurt ourselves. An understanding of the workings of the system can help us not only prevent this but also fix it if need be.

The five elements that form our world are Earth, Water, Fire, Air and Ether, going from the gross to the subtle. Too much of any of these elements can cause a spate of problems ranging from disease to brain fog to financial problems.

# What are these 'Elements'?

Ancient cultures in Greece, Egypt, Babylonia, Tibet, Japan and India have used the five elements to facilitate easier understanding of the nature and complexity of matter.

However, to imagine there is the element of fire in your table or that the element of water can make you emotional may seem a bit bizarre to the uninitiated. Just as physics and chemistry separate the world into various elements, Ayurveda separates everything in the material world on the basis of the five elements. They are not physical objects but esoteric principles. So, to translate them into English and arrive at Earth, Water, Fire, Air and Ether means some of the essence is lost in translation, and we have to make space for that in our understanding.

Take for instance, the element of fire. It doesn't imply the fire we create, but the warmth that is characteristic of most life. This also means that the fire we see and use is not just the fire element alone, but a combination of elements that make its physical manifestation possible. Thoughts, words, actions, things, foods, and our senses are all manifestations of the five elements with a possible predominance of one element.

These five elements can be considered to be the building blocks of all creation. In the body, they are associated with tissues, organs and functions. In the mind, they bring about personality traits and patterns of thinking. In relationships, they represent the equation and connection between two individuals.

# Why Work with the Elements'?

The knowledge of these five elements is well integrated with the principles of Ayurveda, the ancient Indian system of healing. However, the role of these elements extends much further than the physical body alone and warrants our attention.

Normally, people either look at the physical and study the healing of the body on the physical realm, or work with their intuition and heal through energy and the mind. So we often have those who are highly knowledgeable, but are guided by theory in healing, unable to listen to the demands of their own systems or the systems of the clients. Then there are those who are intuitive, listening to and responding to the needs of the body intuitively. Even when people learn both, the two methods remain mostly mutually exclusive in terms of functioning.

The concept of the five elements allows energy healers to bring about a merging these two aspects. Intuition can guide one towards what is wrong, and knowledge can help with getting more clarity as well as in arriving at a more effective solution.

# Some Scientific Perspectives

Much of the discussion on non-physical phenomena is highly debatable in the scientific community, seldom ever reaching a conclusion. Science obviously does not consider the five elements to be 'elements' – indeed we use the word for the sake of convenience; they are not physical elements but principles. Over time, there have been a few scientists who have found some validity in these ideas.

Mathematicians have been fascinated for many centuries with the symmetricity in natural structures. Several natural patterns have been discovered that can be arrived at with mathematical formulae, the Fibonacci spiral, for instance.

The Greek philosopher Plato was also captivated by the order and structure of the material world, and wrote about polyhedrons – now named after him as Platonic solids – in his work Timaeus around 360BC. He associated a solid each with one of the (then studied) four classical elements, associating vaguely the fifth with 'the constellations of the whole heaven'. It was much later that Aristotle associated a fifth element *aithēr* (ether) with 'the Heavens'.

When we follow certain rules, such as all faces must be the same shape, all edges the same length, only one angle throughout the shape and all points touch the edges of a sphere perfectly, only 5 geometric forms are possible. These are the Platonic solids.

The father of Geometry, Euclid of Alexandria, described these solids in complete detail in his work 'The Elements'.

Tetrahedron

Four faces

**Fire**

Cube

Six faces

**Earth**

Octahedron

Eight faces

**Air**

Dodecahedron

Twelve faces

**Water**

Icosahedron

Twenty faces

**Ether**

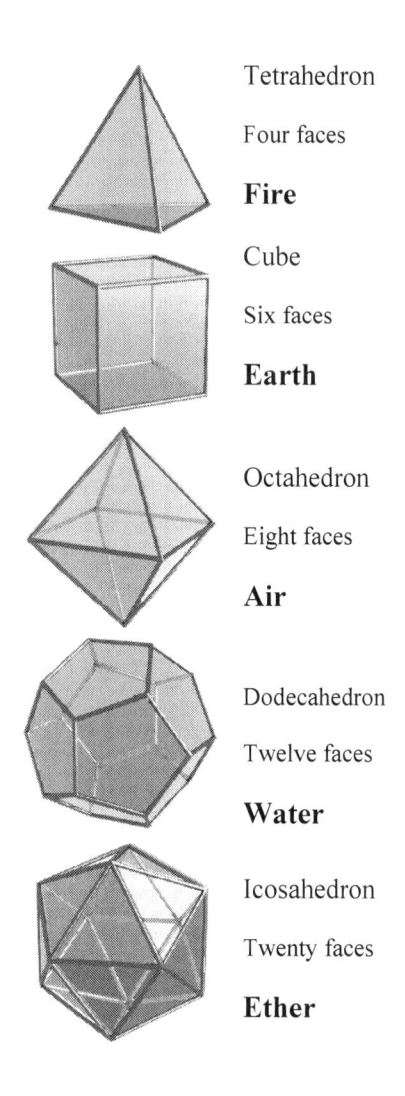

Much later in the 20th century, nuclear physicist Robert Moon attempted to link the Platonic solids to the physical world through the electron shell model. He believed that protons are located at the vertices of a nested structure of four of the five Platonic solid and created a periodic table where the elements were listed in 'octaves' based on the atomic structure[1]. This completes the connection, in a way, between the material world and the concept of the elements, although there may be much more to it than we know yet.

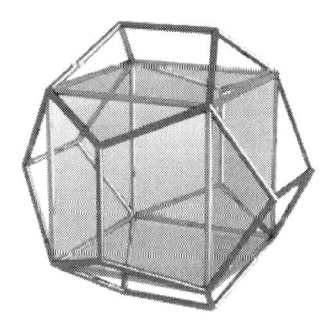

# AKASH (ETHER/ SPACE)

*The day science begins to study non-physical phenomena, it will make more progress in one decade than in all the previous centuries of its existence.*
~ *Nicola Tesla, who discovered zero-point energy*

That which encompasses everything, the vast emptiness, the void, are what *Ākāsh* roughly translates to. This is the first, and the subtlest of all elements: primordial, unmanifest matter. It contains everything, acting like the canvas upon which all of creation can be painted, and has no properties other than mere vibration – resonating with the sound of '*Om*'.

Just hearing the words ether or space inspire a feeling of stillness and vast openness. *Ākāsh* represents freedom of movement and gaps and hollow cavities.

Seldom do we pause to ponder that matter is hardly what it seems. 99.99% of an atom is just space. All of humanity is hung up on the remaining 0.01%! One might wonder what the role of 'space' could be in a discussion on matter, but where would one put matter, if there was no 'space' to place it in? Space is therefore quite an integral part of a discussion on matter.

Unlike the other elements, ether is characterised more by what it is not, rather than what it is. It is clear (absence of visibility), light (absence of weight), dry (absence of moisture), cold (absence of heat), subtle (intangible) and immeasurable, and the actions associated with it are expansion, vibration and non-resistance.

Obviously, on the mental plane this implies expansion of one's horizons and a flexible world-view. Space brings with it an openness to life and to new experiences, and also the ability to move on and leave past baggage in the past.

Within the body, *ākāsh* represents the empty spaces – the hollowness within the intestines, blood vessels, bladder and lungs. The sensory organ that *ākāsh* represents is the ear through which we perceive sound, and the related body part is the mouth. In the chakra system, ether is the element of the throat chakra.

The season associated with ether is winter. The leaves have fallen, the earth is barren and everything is empty and cold, devoid of warmth. In the cycle of life, ether represents death. The body disintegrates and the spirit expands, moving beyond the boundaries of the body.

Metaphysically, ether represents a still, undisturbed mind – vast, formless, impossible to contain, and pregnant with limitless possibilities.

A person with a healthy *Ākāsh* element will be relaxed and detached, and capable of seeing the other's perspective easily. Communication with others will be easy and effective as a result of being able to present one's own views without too much attachment, as well as being able to listen to the opposing views without feeling threatened or taking it personally.

People with a healthy and balanced *Ākāsh* make good healers, being capable of providing a 'healing space' for the client to release and let go of everything that doesn't serve them any longer.

The body is also comfortable with emptiness, and elimination is easy and effective, leading to a healthy amount of sweating, urination and excretion.

# Imbalance: Causes and Consequences

For someone on the path of raja yoga, the goal is often to merge into the void, so such a person might not suffer much from an excess of ether. But for most people, an excess of this element can create severe lack in their lives. Too much space, too much emptiness makes people uneasy, depressed and lacklustre. It makes lives devoid of prosperity and material success. It impacts health by creating severe imbalances in weight, and affecting the voice or the throat.

In an increasingly material world where consumerism is almost a norm, relationships are becoming more and more shallow, and foods are less nutritious than ever before. We consume, but we rarely nourish. Our social media timelines are full of beautiful pictures with our loved ones, but those are probably the only moments we have spent with them – the real, dependable, trusted and full-of-love relationships are fast disappearing. We spend hours reading meaningless and likely false information online, but don't have time to read books that transform. We travel for excitement, but forget to stop and smell the flowers. The lack of emotional, mental and physical nourishment in our lives leaves a gaping void – an excess of the ether element.

However, when we look closer at life, we always find excesses accompanied by deprivation. This excess of space creates a terrifying void – one which we seek to fill, unfortunately with all the wrong things. While we suffer from too much space, we also suffer from too less. We leave our minds no space to rest – we need to constantly think, so much that even a 15 minute bus ride warrants the use of a phone. We need to fill our houses with things, many of which we do not need. We need to meet people, go shopping, travel, do everything, just so that we can pretend that the void isn't there.

A severe imbalance of the *ākāsh* element is often what successful and rich people suffer from the most. They have everything, except space. And this is almost a contagious disease due to the consumerist culture that pervades our society today, so much that people even try to 'fill' their lives with spiritual ideas and objects.

In the absence of enough space, we don't have the 'space' to receive ideas and opinions that diverge from ours. We find it impossible to accommodate others when they need some space, whether emotionally or physically. Healers with an excess of *ākāsh* will attract and take up toxic energies from a client, and in extreme cases all the time, like in a crowd or while meeting friends.

The body responds to excess space by trying to hold on to stuff that should otherwise be eliminated, leading to problems like constipation. Too little space in the body might cause the body to try to eliminate too much, causing dehydration or excessive motions.

## Balancing *Ākāsh*

While space itself is devoid of nourishment, a seed can only sprout in an empty land – so requisite space is critical for growth and nourishment. Balancing this element would need us to create space in the right ways. Fasting, slowing down, meditation and silence can help greatly in bringing the ether element into balance.

**Relationships**: The importance of the right amount of space in relationships cannot be overstated. While too much can create distance and an eventual end, too little space in a relationship can also stifle it to death. Ensuring some time apart or activities that you enjoy outside of the relationship can help to balance the problem of swinging back and forth from too much attachment to repulsion.

Ether also represents sound, and being associated with the throat chakra, it brings in the element of communication. It is no secret that healthy communication is the foundation of a good relationship. If things are difficult, one exercise if both participants are willing, could be having a timer and each person speaking freely for 5 minutes without being interrupted by the other person. Of course, decency has to be maintained and both are only allowed to speak about how they feel, without blaming or deliberately hurting the other person.

**Lifestyle**: One of the biggest reasons why meditation helps so many people is because it means people spend a few minutes doing nothing. Sparing some time every week when you do absolutely nothing goes a long way in balancing the space element. If you have a garden, that is a nice place to relax, and if you have access to a park or a forest nearby, grab a mat and spend some time relaxing. Note that trekking through a forest is not the same as simply spending time doing nothing – and doing nothing means you do not sit there trying to connect with nature – because even that trying is action. Just relax, and do nothing.

*Ākāsh* slowly increases in the body as we age, warranting a change in eating patterns and general lifestyle. The healthiest people are those who gradually start reducing the quantity of their food as they age, as this helps their system remain in sync with the change. Reducing 'heavy' activities like shouldering big responsibilities and letting the younger ones take charge, along with practicing gentle and compassionate detachment helps people integrate this change the most gracefully.

**Work**: Creation needs space, and too much of work can diminish not just mental capacity but also your problem-solving skills and passion for work. Too much of a good thing is not so helpful – and this must especially be borne in mind by those who work for themselves. While those who work for others are driven by external pressures, those who work for themselves can sometimes be much more driven and prone to over-working without ever realising it.

By asking yourself a few questions might help, like: is this really as important as I pretend this is? Is this really more important than the things I have been putting off? Is this really just a short busy stint like I promised myself or has it been stretching out for too long? Am I using my work to avoid another uncomfortable situation?

If you are working for someone else and being overworked, shorter empty spaces during your day can help you cope better. Take 2 or 5 minute breaks where you do nothing, 2-3 times during the day. If that seems too long, even a few seconds of getting up, stretching, palming the eyes and becoming still can help.

## Meditating on *Ākāsh*

For people who live in a close knit group where everyone knows each other, and who work in the fields or do other forms of manual labour meditating on space can be very life transforming.

To do this, sit comfortably, preferably in an open space, or at least in your most spacious room, and let your body settle down. Once you are comfortable, tune in to the silence or the space around you, whichever feels right. If you tune in to the silence, you can become aware of the pockets of silence around you even when there is noise outside. If you are tuning in to the space, you can become aware of the pockets of space present in the middle of things. Stay in this awareness for as long as you like, preferably at least 10-15 minutes.

For those who barely know the names of their neighbours, who eat imported foods, spend a lot of time on the internet and tend to be 'spaced out' often, it is best to meditate on the earth element, and if meditating on space at all, meditate on the space *within*.

To do this, sit comfortably, preferably in an open space, or at least in your most spacious room, and let your body settle down. Once you are comfortable, become aware that you are formed by a collection of atoms that are nothing but little things moving about in space. Become aware of the space that your body is filled with. If this is too hard to imagine, you can become aware of the empty space in your throat region, especially during the pause in your breathing. Just remain in that awareness for as long as you are comfortable, preferably at least 10-15 minutes. There may be a tendency to cough during this process but that is just your body trying to throw out blockages, so let it happen.

**Breathing Exercise**: *Ujjayi pranayama:* Sit comfortably with your spine erect. Take a long, deep breath through your nostrils, contracting your throat as you do this so that there is a hissing sound in your throat and the breath becomes long and thin. Now exhale slowly through the nose. Do this three times and no more.

After a week of practice, you can take it deeper by first inhaling as outlined, and then 'locking' your throat and touching your chin to your chest (also called the *Jalandhar bandha*). Hold for a maximum of 10 seconds.

Release your chin and straighten your head. Close your right nostril with your right thumb and exhale through the left nostril. Do it thrice to start with, and slowly you can work your way up to a maximum of eleven times.

This exercise improves focus and improves spinal health. It slows the body down, slowing the heartbeat and the blood supply to the brain, and eventually allowing you to feel the stillness in your body. It greatly supports meditative practices, and also heals thyroid problems. It is great for the voice, and very beneficial for singers and speakers who tend to strain their voice.

# VAYU (AIR)

*A breath of fresh air is a great thing to take,
and an even better thing to be.*
*~ Anon*

Ether does not dense enough to facilitate the creation of form. Creation first needs some sort of friction, some contraction and expansion. So as ether becomes denser, heavier and less subtle, it becomes air, the second of the five great elements.

The predominant characteristic of air is its motion. It represents kinetic energy, and initiates and directs movement. It is the basis of all contact and exchange, and of all the gravitational, magnetic and electric fields. This element is mobile, clear, sharp, dry, light, rough, cold, subtle and hard (due to its drying nature).

When we think of air, we instantly associate it with breath. The lack of this element will kill us faster than the lack of any other element. It is the foundation of all life, and is synonymous with *prāna*, life force energy. In *Sānkhya* philosophy, *vāyu* is divided into five categories based on the direction of movement, *prāna* (inward moving); *vyāna* (outward moving); *udāna* (upward moving), *apāna* (downward moving), and *samāna* (a balancing and stabilizing force that pulls matter toward the center).

In the body, aliveness comes from the air element itself. This is the force that enables breathing to happen, the blood to circulate, the nerve impulses to travel, and the joints to move smoothly.

Air brings with it the sense of touch. Since it evolves from ether, it also carries the property of sound, so we can hear the wind, as well as feel its touch. The sensory organ associated with air is obviously our skin, through which we perceive sensations and pressure, and the related body part is the hands. In the chakra system, air is the element of the heart chakra – isn't it therefore natural that the deepest experience of love for most people is through the touch of a compassionate person?

The season associated with air is autumn. Nature moves from flowering and bearing fruits into lightness and preparation for the winter. In the cycle of life too, *vāyu* represents the transitional period following the most productive years of our life, as head towards the winter of life itself. Women transition through menopause, men through a desire for retirement – a desire for lightness, for a letting go of past baggage and responsibilities.

Metaphysically, air represents the flow of thoughts in the mind and a sense of freedom. When in balance, *vāyu* facilitates quick thinking.

## Imbalance: Causes and Consequences

Air needs freedom and space to move. However, too much desire for space can create dryness and lack of nourishment – both physically and emotionally. When we are too focussed on safeguarding our freedom – whether freedom of speech or freedom of action – in life or in relationships, with a disregard to the pain others might have to experience as a result of this, it causes physical as well as emotional manifestations of *vāyu* imbalance.

Too much movement also increases *vāyu* in our system. Unfortunately, our lifestyles are today defined by movement. We travel more than ever before. We almost live on the internet, a tool that makes the mind fly to various parts of the world and from one topic to another, fleeting and rarely ever settling on anything. We multi-task, again encouraging the mind to continuously shift from one thing to another. We're hooked onto junk foods, which further send our *vāyu* out of balance or we're too obsessed with 'healthy eating', depriving our bodies of nourishing comfort foods. People either don't exercise at all, or exercise too much.

Disturbances in the air element can create problems in circulation. It may be moving too fast, too slow, or might get blocked.

When in excess, *vāyu* can bring about excessive thinking and an incapacity to sit still and take life as it comes. This is typically associated with anxiety, restlessness, forgetfulness and sleeplessness. When the imbalance is moderate, people have trouble concentrating and are lost in their thoughts, unable to even follow a conversation, let alone a book, without losing their train of thought. They just build one castle in the air after another but never actually taking action to manifest their dreams. Extreme or prolonged imbalance can leave people feeling highly strung, as if they can never calm down, or cause nervous breakdowns. In its extreme, it can cause mental instability, chronic depression, blackouts or delirium.

Physically, it can create too much movement in the body: blood flowing too rapidly can cause palpitations and hypertension, too much air in the digestive system will cause diarrhoea, and in the joints it causes hypermobility. If too extreme, it can cause premature aging, convulsions, fibromyalgia, etc.

If the air is moving too slowly it causes sluggishness, laziness, dullness, drowsiness and a very slowly responding mind. Physically it can cause poor circulation, constipation or sluggish motion - irritable bowel syndrome if extreme, and slow moving joints.

A blockage in the flow of air in the body can cause what we often refer to as 'brain fog' – an incapacity to think. Physically it can cause the blood supply is cut off with potentially catastrophic consequences, severe constipation, frozen joints, etc.

As I've mentioned before, imbalance often means too much on the one hand and too less on the other. So while the body might display an imbalance towards excess *vāyu* in some symptoms, other symptoms might indicate a deprivation.

Problems in digestion can eventually lead to weight problems, either too much or too less weight. An unsteady mind can create problems in decision-making, and too much imbalance can cause a person to shift too frequently –from one job/ home/ relationship to another, or to stagnate in one place in life.

## Balancing *Vāyu*

Air needs freedom to move, but too much movement can dry the system up and create problems. So to maintain *vāyu* in balance, control is needed so as to prevent excess flow along with requisite freedom to prevent stagnation.

While our lifestyles in general make us very prone to imbalances in *vāyu*, extra care must be taken during autumn and during *vāyu* phases of life to ensure that it remains in balance.

**Relationships**: Air is about control and freedom, and this is very relevant to relationships. We like control, but too much control stifles and destroys a relationship. Too little involvement and people drift apart. Engaging to the right extent is a lesson that can only be learned over time, but if there is a focus on learning how to reach the right level of engagement, this can be achieved much faster.

Traveling together, especially on slow, unplanned journeys or picnics can be very healing if the relationship has become too 'cold'. Since air brings the element of touch, learning to caress the other with love, and maybe learning to lovingly massage your partner can bring in deep healing and connection. In other relationships, the power of a rightly-timed hug is incomparable.

**Lifestyle**: Structure is the secret to balanced air in your system. Exercises is a very important aspect of our lives, but as mentioned before, people tend to do too less or too much. Learning where to draw the line and bringing in the discipline to have at least a few minutes of exercise daily goes a long way in bringing about a balance. Fast-moving exercises aimed at burning calories often hurt the air element in the body. Slow exercises practiced with awareness and without distractions like music can help bring about balance. Breathing exercises like *pranayama* also help a lot in balancing the *vāyu* in the body.

It is important to bear in mind that the air element increases and can get aggravated easily during phases in our life where we are undergoing a transition. So if you are in the process of moving to another city or to another job, or even into another relationship or having a baby, these are times of intense transitions and if some energy is spent in taking care to balance *vāyu* through nourishing foods and a structured routine to the extent possible, it will ensure that the transition is as painless as possible. If your job involves a lot of traveling or a lot of thinking, or even if you spend the whole day working in an air conditioned office, the same rules apply.

Emotionally, resistance to life situations creates imbalances in *vāyu* and surrender is the antidote that helps accept life as it is. Learning to surrender to life starts letting the body and mind relax and with progress in this direction, a lot of physical and mental problems get resolved by themselves.

**Work**: Simple things like clearing the mess on your desk out can remove *vāyu* imbalances. Resistance also creates imbalance, so if you frequently have to do work that you dislike, or dislike your job altogether but cannot quit, seek therapeutic help to heal your emotions towards your work.

If your work schedule involves a lot of varied action plans, that can increase the air element and reduce your efficiency. Bear in mind that multi-tasking increases *vāyu* and reduces your capacity to implement. Bring focus only to one task at a time, and close all the irrelevant windows on your computer and/ or tabs on your browser. Consciously think about only the task at hand, and not others, unless of course that is how your work needs you to function. Organising your schedule and tasks will help you accomplish a lot more.

## Meditating on *Vāyu*

Wear loose, comfortable clothes and if possible, sit in an airy, open space. It is even better if you can feel or hear the breeze. If you are in the open and can feel the movement of air, do the entire meditation mentioned below. If not, skip the first step.

Take a comfortable position and let your body relax. Allow yourself to become aware of the sensation of the breeze touching your skin. If your clothes are moving in the breeze, become aware of those sensations too. Allow yourself to become one with the breeze, let go of your focus on your body. Continue for about 5 minutes.

Next, allow your focus to come to your breath. Raise your shoulders as you breathe in, and let them fall to the normal position as you breathe out. Maintain your awareness during this phase, on the movement of air in your nostrils.

Now breathe through your chest – let your chest expand when you breathe in, and fall when you breathe out. Maintain your awareness in your chest area when you do this. Continue for a few minutes.

Breathe through your belly. Let your stomach expand as you breathe in, and contract as you breathe out. This should come naturally as you shift the focus of breathing from chest to belly but if not, it is ok to gently create this movement till it comes naturally.

Once this movement comes naturally, just remain watching the movement of the belly as it moves with your breath, remaining aware of the movement of air in your belly region if possible. Allow all of your attention to flow to this area of your body and relax completely. Remain in this state for 10 minutes or so if you have the time.

Gently get up when you are ready, and if possible, avoid the use of the internet, loud music or gossiping after this meditation so that you can sustain the effect for as long as possible.

**Breathing Exercise**: *Nadi shodhan pranayama:* Sit comfortably with your spine erect. Close your right nostril with your right thumb, and inhale. Now close your left nostril with your ring finger and exhale. Pause, and inhale. Close your right nostril now, and exhale. Continue for 5-10 minutes.

This is a very balancing *pranayama* and can be done for longer if needed. It balances the two hemispheres of the brain and clears the subtle energy channels (*nadis*) in our body. It normalizes the pulse rate (P) and systolic and diastolic blood pressure.

# TEJAS/ AGNI (FIRE)

*I survived because the fire inside me burned brighter than the fire around me.*
*~ Joshua Graham*

When the friction of air is intense enough, it leads to the formation of heat and fire, the third of the great elements. The generation of heat gives rise to the capacity for transmutation from one element to another. This is the energy that allows fruits to ripen, the fruits on the tree, the fruits of our labor, as well as the fruits of our spiritual *sadhana*.

The predominant characteristics of *agni* are heat and light. The sun is the generator of energy for the earth, while our internal fire is the generator of energy in our bodies. It is hot, sharp, intense, dry, light, subtle, clear and soft. Agni is the principle behind all sources of energy in the world, from solar to hydroelectric, fossil fuel, nuclear and even bio-diesel. It is classified into *jala agni* (ordinary fire), *vaidyuta agni* (electric fire) and *saura agni* (solar fire).

As it carries with it the property of sound and touch from ether and air, fire possesses the capacity to be heard and felt, and it brings with it a third property – to be seen. Thus obviously, the sense organ related to this element is the eyes. Fire provides the light that makes perception possible, and eyes are the instrument that absorb this information. Therefore, most disorders related to the eyes are a result of the imbalance of *agni* in the body.

The body part related to *agni* is the feet, since they are the center of heat in the body. If you've observed, cooling the feet during hot weather cools the body down, and simply cold feet during winters and prevent good sleep! Metaphysically, the feet represent the direction of one's life – physically one would use the feet to determine not only the direction but also the speed at which we move in that direction. Determining the direction and the intensity with which we choose to take action are both characteristics of the fire element. The chakra associated with this element is the *Manipura*, the solar plexus.

Fire burns away impurities, and a good, strong fire can protect one from negative energy and psychic attacks. A weak fire leaves a person open to receiving and retaining harmful energies and entities.

*Tejas* also means radiance or illumination. This element brings vitality not just to the physical body but also the mind. A person with a healthy fire element is confident, warm, friendly, energetic and driven and has the strength and vision to handle power correctly. Such people make great leaders, fair and honest and capable of changing the world.

The season related to this element is obvious summer. This is a time when the heat of the sun comes down in all its intensity, warming the earth and providing fire for action. This is the time of the year when the activity of not just the humans, but also of the plants and animals reach their peak. If the heat is not too intense, this is a great time to implement all the plans made during the mentally fertile times of autumn and winter.

In the cycle of life, *agni* represents our most productive years, the ones just after our youth. This is a phase where action is the most intense, on the work front as well as the personal front. It is our time to live out our dharma.

# Imbalance: Causes and Consequences

Too much heat in life sets our *agni* out of balance. Emotionally, this means intense agitation, or allowing anger to take over our life and too much ambition. At work, too much focus and intensity will create an imbalance.

Ideally, one can perform all duties while still remaining relaxed. But as we haven't be taught how to do this, a lot of us have a tendency to try to get motivated to do something. Motivation in most cases involves a rush of adrenaline, and this also increases the heat in the body. If you try to ignite passion all the time to facilitate your actions, then you are going to end up with a fire that will start to consume your body instead of nourish it.

Unfortunately, as this has become our standard approach to life, so much that companies pay huge amounts of money to motivational speakers that come to bring some life into otherwise exhausted and demotivated employees, that we are addicted to this adrenaline rush. As a result political as well as other campaigns that incite feelings of anger and hatred are far more successful. Exposure to these sort of ideas day in and day out is hurting our internal fire, creating both short term as well as long term damage.

Intense spiritual *sadhana* can also intensify the fire in the body and cause various ailments. Fire is that which transmutes, and just like ether becomes air which then becomes fire through intense friction, intense meditation can take one from a state of silence to facing the noise and resistance within one's mind, and when this crosses a point, it ignites into fire that starts to burn the body. Up to a certain point, this fire is transformational and transmutes our emotional and mental impurities to love and compassion, but there is a very thin line here and most people end up with at least a mild form of *agni* imbalance during a spiritual retreat.

Too much heat in the body leads to bloodshot eyes and flushed skin, excessive sweating, often with a sour smell, an acidic stomach, excessive urination and bowel movement, inflamed tissues, fever, skin rashes, early graying and digestion and liver problems. The body might often feel very hot, and the person is comfortable in cold weather, feeling highly agitated in hot weather. The person is too energetic for his/ her own good and can end up over-straining.

Emotionally too much *agni* leads to a person becoming extremely vain, self-critical, agitated, judgmental and demanding perfectionism from others, giving unsolicited advice, bullying, obsessed and having tunnel vision.

Excessive fire for too long can lead a person to a burnout, after which the fire may be too weak. If a person has a tendency to suppress anger and hatred, addicted to the idea of being a *good person*, then also the fire becomes too weak. If a person is almost never angry, it is usually a clear sign of weak *agni*.

If the fire is too weak, the skin turns pale, clotting of the blood slows down as does the rate of healing, the blood is impure, digestion and absorption are weak and the person feels cold easily. As the body desperately tries to hold on to heat, sweating, urination and bowel movements reduce drastically. The person has very little stamina and feels tired and sleeps more than needed.

Emotionally, a weak fire reduces a person's capacity to comprehend new information. The person loses touch with personal power and feels traumatized by the anger expressed by others, and needs people to 'express things in the right way' to be able to function. Frequently, such people will attract people who abuse them, as nature tries to force them to get in touch with their own power and learn to stand up for themselves. Their energy levels are low and drive and ambition are minimal.

# Balancing Agni

Too much air can blow fire out of proportion or blow it out altogether, and too much water or earth can extinguish it while in the right proportion they nourish the fire. When out of control, *agni* can burn our system down, and when too feeble, our systems can struggle to stay alive.

During summers and during highly active phases of our lives, we need to take special care to ensure that we don't burn out or get too focused and intense.

**Relationships**: Here are a few questions that can help you determine if there is too much fire in your relationship:

- Is your partner (or other family member) always unreasonable, unreliable and disappointing you?
- Is the other person too dependent on you?
- Do you find yourself shouting or getting angry often?
- Do you have any occasional or frequent desire for revenge or to teach the other a lesson they need to learn?

If the answer to the above questions is yes, then there is too much *agni* affecting your relationship. On the other hand, if you find that you are always disappointing the other, too dependent on the other person, if you try to manipulate the other to do as you wish, if you're not able to express your pain or fears to the other, always feeling like you are not good enough, it means your emotional fire is weak.

If the fire is too strong, awareness would be the first step. When out of control, fire burns, and can leave the others in the relationship wounded. However, nobody wants to come face to face with the fact that we have hurt someone, and this can cause many to just pretend that it was the other person's fault. In addition to everything, people with a very strong fire are actually very action-oriented and will do a lot for their loved ones – an overpowered fire will burn up the water in the body, and the person tries to compensate for the lack of nourishment through action and responsibility – so fire people actually do a lot for their families and loved ones, but it still leaves the other people feeling 'burned' and not 'feeling' the love. Since a person with excess fire starts defining love as action, they then start getting upset that they are not getting enough love in return, because others do far less for them. This creates a frustration which comes out as anger and power struggles, further taking away any scope for nourishment. People with too much fire are often isolated in their families and feel that everyone else is a team and they are left out.

If you have said yes to more than two questions above, start meditating on whether you are trying to change the other person to suit your preferences. Fire is illumination, the light of awareness, and more often than not, simply awareness is enough to resolve the problem.

If the fire is too weak, then a lot of self-work is required to get reconnected with one's inner power. Again, awareness is key, and a regular spiritual practice and grounding are a must. Fire can be weak due to insufficient wood (earth element), insufficient fuel (earth+ water element) or insufficient air or space. Depending on the root cause, the solution needs to be implemented.

In general, a simple exercise to balance power issues in a relationship can be to look into each other's eyes. Often during power struggles, the memory of love disappears. Looking into each other's eyes for about 10 minutes every day without talking and preferably without thinking about other things can bring about a deep healing and balance into the relationship. If possible, you can also try to harmonize the breath while doing this.

**Lifestyle**: People with too much fire need constant action, and usually focused action at that. These people benefit tremendously by learning to relax and do unimportant, unplanned things. However, this does not come naturally and cannot be forced on them. If a person with excessive fire takes it upon himself to balance his lifestyle, do-nothing vacations by the sea or lake-side where there is time for leisurely swims or time to sit in a forest will help bring balance. Or you can set a day or half in a week where you do nothing, just relax. If this is too hard, art can provide the middle ground, and participating in art classes, preferably pottery or abstract painting without trying to achieve perfection can help considerably.

Cooling breathing exercises (*pranayama)* and cold showers also help in the short term, and regular meditation can bring about lasting change for the better, even healing physical ailments like high blood pressure.

When out of check, *agni* radiates outwards from a person and hurts other people. The universe often compensates for these unconscious pain inflicted on others through bringing the person some sort of loss. Charity helps to change this, and if it involves actions instead of just monetary donations, it will be far more effective and beneficial. However, this must be done with the attitude of service, since a strong fire element also often tends to make a person push their help onto others – remember that learning to listen to the other person's need is a critical part of being able to help. Unsolicited advice must be avoided.

If you live with a person who has excessive fire, trying to force them to relax will only cause greater friction and an increased fire. In such a case, approach *agni* balance through food, and prepare the food with total awareness of the love you have for this person.

People with a weak fire will benefit by joining martial arts classes, especially the Asian styles, since they are more focused on progressing through a balanced solar plexus energy. Many with a weak fire will feel extreme resistance towards joining such an activity, but sustaining it for a few months can be life-transforming. Working on getting in touch with one's own power is also essential, but combining this with martial arts classes brings the fastest progress in my experience.

**Work**: Balance needs equal amounts of each element. So in a team, different people bring in different aspects of the element. The dreamer for example, might not be the most reliable one, while the most efficient member might shy away from any communication. Excessive fire creates an expectation of perfectionism, bringing about a frustration with those not living up to our expectations. This can compromise the potential of the team and sour relationships. Also, excessive *agni* can lead a person to take on more than their system can comfortably handle, compromising their health and balance in life. As mentioned before, bringing in awareness and consciously practicing acceptance and not taking action when there is a desire to do more, can help a person balance the fire element at work.

Too little fire can cause a loss of passion for work, and a lack of challenge in the work environment can reduce the fire as well. Acceptance is the key again, and learning to rekindle the passion within by reminding oneself that one does not have to grow and be challenged all the time, and that sometimes rest periods are great for bringing in fresh energy.

## Meditating on *Agni*

**If you have too much *agni*:**

Sit comfortably in a quiet place and begin by taking a few deep breaths. Become aware of your body and imagine that it is on fire, starting in the solar plexus and radiating outwards. If your body generally feels hot or if you are feeling anger in that moment, imagine this heat or anger coming from this fire. Feel this fire burning you, hurting you.

Once you feel this, imagine a gentle, loving rain soothing and calming your body. Imagine it slowly extinguishing all of the fire except a small ball of fire in your solar plexus. Sit with this feeling of gentle rain still touching and cooling your body, and being aware of this small soothing and healing ball of fire within your belly. Stay this way for at least 10 minutes, and then open your eyes when you're ready. If you do this just before you go out for a walk in the park or just before a relaxed day, it will help you even more. Do not follow this meditation with TV time or anything else that could potentially agitate you, if you want to maximize its effect.

**Breathing Exercise**: If you have trouble sleeping due to excessive *agni* and find yourself staying up at night thinking and planning, breathe through the left nostril 21 times just before you sleep.

**If you have too little *agni*:**

Sit comfortably in a quiet place and begin by taking a few deep breaths. Become aware of your body and imagine that your body is a balloon, filled with air. Now try to see if you can see where the fire in your body is located. Usually if there is a weak fire, you might find that it has moved to the outer edges of your body, leaving the center empty, or you might find that it is distorted or has moved to another part of your body. If you find this hard to do, imagine that the outer edges of your body are on fire.

As you breathe in, imagine this fire moving from the edges (or wherever else it had moved) and coming closer to the center. Do this until it comes together as a little ball in the center of your solar plexus, bringing it closer with every inhalation.

Next, as you breathe in, let your body absorb energy from your surroundings. When you breathe out, imagine that all the energy that you have absorbed as you inhaled, is going into this flame and expanding it. Keep breathing into this flame until it reaches the size of a tennis ball. Once there, simply be aware of this ball of fire, and remain in this awareness for about 10 minutes. You may slowly open your eyes when you are done.

***Note**: Fire contains within itself the quality of explosiveness. For this reason, it is important that any meditation on fire be done with care. Do not overdo it or exaggerate the exercises outlined in a bid to achieve faster results.*

**Breathing Exercise:** *Bhastrika Pranayama:* Sit comfortably on a chair or cross-legged on the floor and ensure that your spine is erect. Breathe in and breathe out forcefully, letting your lungs expand and be sucked in by the force of it. Breathe through the lungs up to the diaphragm, not through the belly. Stop after 10 rounds or the moment you feel tired, do not overdo. You can slowly increase the number of rounds to 50 if you desire. If you haven't practiced this before, I recommend looking up a video or taking guidance from a yoga teacher.

This exercise is very effective in clearing blockages from the nose and chest, and is also very good for those suffering from asthma and throat infections. It increases the oxygen content in the blood and activates all organs.

# APAS (WATER)

*When they ask you why you love
the rain, the ocean, the river,
tell them it is because
unlike the people
who should have loved you better,
the water was never afraid to touch you;
even when you were
at your most damaged and broken.
~ Nikita Gill*

The first three elements still do not have the capacity to form anything solid. As fire gets denser, it starts to lose its freedom and starts to cool down and form water, the fourth of the great elements.

It develops qualities of cohesion, adhesion and fluidity. Ether, air and fire all move outwards. Water moves inwards – it binds, holds things together, just as loose soil can come together into a ball when mixed with a little water. Water thus facilitates construction and helps structures form and bind together. Its qualities are cloudy, cool, wet, flowing, soft, dull, stable, heavy and sticky.

Unlike the expansive and upward-moving first three elements, water is downward-moving and facilitates contraction.

When one thinks of water, one thinks of the feeling of drinking a glass of water to quench thirst – that burning created by excess fire. For this reason, we find that a burning ambition rarely co-exists with a deeply satisfying relationship. No matter what vessel water is placed in, its upper surface remains at the same level throughout. Water brings balance to our body, mind, priorities and life, and obviously plays a significant role in bringing the five elements into balance.

While fire transmutes and leaves no trace of itself, water retains information. Recent scientific studies[2] are showing that water has memory and as water travels it picks up and stores information from all of the places that it has travelled through – the journey makes microscopic changes to the its molecules. Water holds on – not just in the physical plane, but also across the thread of time. It is thus also responsible for our memory.

Water contains the property of taste, along with the properties of the first three elements. So we can hear the sound of flowing water, we can feel its wetness and its temperature, and we can also taste it. Indeed, without water, taste is impossible – one cannot taste anything if the mouth is dry and there is no saliva. The sense organ related to this element is thus obviously the tongue. Disorders of the ability to taste are thus a sign of imbalance of *apas*.

Given that water relates to nourishment, and that the related sense is taste, is it any wonder then, that the most powerful memories related to the love of the mother are often related to food? It is not a myth that the way to the heart goes through the stomach. Nourishing, loving food straightaway takes one back to the memories of love experienced from one's mother.

The tongue is also associated with speech and expression, so water is also associated with a joyful and spontaneous expression of the self, through words, music, dance and art.

The body part related to this element is the urethra, the organ that releases waste water from the human body and creates balance. The quality and frequency of urination can tell a lot about the *apas* imbalance in the body. The chakra associated with this element is the *Swadisthana*, the sacral chakra.

Water also lubricates, protects and cleanses. It protects the body from burning through too much fire, against the roughness and motion of air and the dissolution of ether. It combines with earth, forming mucous and coating various sensitive membranes in the body and protecting them from friction and dryness.

Water is influenced by the moon and is constantly fluctuating through tides. We imagine tides to be something expansive, something that happens in the oceans, but there are microscopic tides in a tea-cup too, as there are in our bodies which are approximately 70% water. These tides give rise to emotions.

The primary emotion related to water is fear; since water creates cohesiveness – dependency – there is a fear of instability and loss. It is no surprise that one of the most common fears we find are that of water. Fire hurts people far more frequently and harshly, but rarely do we find people with a phobia of fire. But we all know at least one person that fears water.

Usually opposites come from the same source – and the opposite of fear would be courage, which is also a quality that *apas* brings to our lives. In a sense, the opposite of fear would also be relaxation and enjoyment, which are also areas that this element is responsible for. Water ensures we are able to participate, engage and enjoy the beautiful moments of our lives. This includes enjoyment of food, as well as sexuality.

Some scientists believe that life evolved from the comforts of the sea onto to the harshness of land as a result of tides[3]. The changing levels of water pushed living beings onto land, and they had to learn to adapt, learning to eventually walk and procreate on land[4]. *Apas* does the same with us, pushing us, but gently enough to enable us to move out of our comfort zone and push forward and grow.

The season associated with *apas* is spring. It is the season when the snow melts and nourishes the earth with water, allowing life to spring forth. In the cycle of life, water represents our time of learning. As it is the element of cohesion, these are the years we spend accumulating knowledge, tools and the patience needed to live out our dharma through the fiery *agni* years of our life.

For women, periods and pregnancy are also times when the water element is predominant, and extra care needs to be taken so that the system does not go out of balance during this time.

# Imbalance: Causes and Consequences

Most of our world is becoming increasingly materialistic, leaving little space for emotional freedom. Children are often told to 'behave themselves' and watch their parents suppress their own emotions as they grow up. The consequence is that most people grow up with no idea how to handle their emotions. In the face of an intense emotional moment – whether joyous or painful – the learned behavior is to suppress. People learn to cope through either over-reaction and manipulation or through shutting down and pretending they are not vulnerable. This along with suppressed sexuality is a potent combination for severe water imbalances in the system.

Water nourishes and protects, so an imbalance in the body will affect the way a person receives physical, emotional and financial nourishment. Too much *apas* leaves a person widely fluctuating like the tides, and too little will leave a person dry and parched not just physically but in other ways too.

Water also absorbs. When a person has abundant water element along with a slightly weak fire (purification), the system absorbs negativity from the surroundings, including family members, teachers, friends, colleagues, etc. Since water flows just as freely with or without impurities, people with this quality can flow with life nevertheless, but this affects them by taking away clarity, focus and their ability to deeply nourish. Such people also often have ample but soft fat all over their body or in specific areas if only certain emotions are being accumulated.

The flowing nature of water is great when in balance – it allows a person to flow with life, taking uncertainties and obstacles in their stride, 'flowing' around them through the easiest path available. However, when this is out of balance, people can be too accommodating, prone to getting bullied, pushed around and manipulated.

Water can also change form – it can freeze or turn into steam based on the level of heat available. Often, when people are unable to handle extreme emotions, they freeze. However, ice does not support life – fire is needed, so the body tries to compensate by raising the fire levels. This creates a unique imbalance, creating a 'fire and ice' effect in the system. Emotionally, this means that a person might generally be unaffected and uninvolved, but might have an outrageous temper that shows up once in a while. Physically this translates to hot and cold areas in the body, where parts of the body might be cold or freezing while others are warm or burning.

The ocean is affected by tides, and when the tides are too strong, it can capsize a boat altogether. The same applies to this element.

If *apas* is too strong in the body, the mind and body become more subjective to the influence of the moon, and the 'tides' can affect life greatly. A person can experience mood swings, women can experience much greater difficulty during periods, and life in general becomes turbulent. Interestingly, tides involve more as well as less water, so the person fluctuates between too much and too little *apas* when things are out of balance.

As water relates to nourishment, a lack of this element can create an intense desire to nourish oneself – through either food, shopping, drugs or sex. So addictions are a common result of *apas* imbalance. Sometimes this addiction can also be emotional, and many times people can find themselves in toxic but highly addictive relationships which they feel they cannot live without. Adequate self-nourishment can completely heal this issue.

The lack of *apas* can bring about a poor memory and an incapacity to feel emotions freely. People become cold and emotionally rigid, or extremely angry and vindictive.

In the body, an increase in *apas* causes an overflow of the water element from the stomach into the circulation and floods the tissues of the body, primarily the plasma (the clear fluid in blood which holds together the red blood cells, white blood cells, and other components), fat and fluidic reproductive tissues. This water retention can affect the body by causing problems like edema (abnormal accumulation of fluid in tissues), fluid build-up in the sinuses or lungs causing infections, runny nose, cough or breathing difficulties, obesity and genital discharge. It also reduces the quality while increasing the quantity of breast milk and menstrual fluids.

Poor levels of *apas* cause the opposite effects. The mucous membranes dry up, lips and eyes are dry, sweating and urination decrease and stools are dry and hard. Dry mouth, dry skin, lack of sweating, lethargy and dizziness are initial symptoms of dehydration caused by lack of water. As the problem gets more serious, it can cause headaches, weakness in muscles, low blood pressure, increased heart rate and even unconsciousness.

# Balancing *Apas*

**Relationships**: A relationship devoid of the water element will be devoid of commitment and potentially at the same time very pleasure-seeking, which might lead the couple to connect with other people or maybe even both agree to have an open relationship. If the water element is too high it will lead to an overly dependent relationship where is too much attachment for their own good and potentially jealousy and over-possessiveness.

What is far more common however, is when one person has too much *apas* and the other too less. This leads to a toxic, addictive relationship. Just like tides go high and low, a partner that satisfies and then disappoints subconsciously reminds oneself of the movement of water. If there is a lack of *apas* in one's system, this can create a great deal of attraction. Eventually nature increases the 'tides' to great intensity – swinging from intense pleasure to highly violent, in a bid to bring the person out of this external addiction and to learn to nourish himself/ herself.

If the relationship is devoid of *apas*, going for couples dance classes, giving each other nourishing massages, and changing the diet to include more *apas*-abundant foods will help.

A rediscovering of love is needed. If both partners have never experienced deep love before and this is the only way they know how to relate, seeking therapy will be the fastest way to heal as this is normally an indication of an emotional shut-down due to childhood or past life trauma. If love has been experienced in the past, it is simply a matter of rekindling it – either in the relationship or oneself. This can be done through practicing kindness, non-judgment, forgiveness, faith and vulnerability.

If there is too much *apas*, then time apart is essential, and spending some time learning to enjoy activities/ hobbies without the presence of the other is deeply therapeutic. Too much leaning on another is a result of not being grounded enough in oneself, and the root cause of this is lack of self-love. So massaging oneself, cooking for oneself, or doing whatever else for oneself that one make one feel loved will help. Hug yourself if you have to!

In addictive relationships it is difficult to bring about balance because usually the one in control has little to gain by bringing balance, and will want to maintain status quo. The addicted one, the one being controlled/ abused needs to work very hard on himself or herself and learn to remain in balance 'through the tides'. Frequently this eventually means walking out of the relationship unless the love is strong enough that the other transforms to prevent the break-up.

The following exercise can help couples balance the water element in all the above cases, and also in situations where the sex-drive is out of sync.

Sit comfortably on a chair or cross-legged, facing your partner. Both place the right hand on the other's heart, and the left hand on top of the partner's right hand, i.e. on one's own chest. Start by closing your eyes and becoming aware of your breath in the heart area, and then tune in to the energy and emotion in your heart. How does it feel? Do you feel love? Heaviness? Pain? Joy? Expansiveness? Constriction? Peace? Just allow yourself to feel this, whatever it is, and do not *think* about it –do not try to explain away the pain, rationalize it, or try to make sense of it. Simply feel it.

When you feel that this is enough, let go of the hands. If the partner is not done yet, wait until he/she is finished. Now open your eyes and look into each other's eyes.

The next phase depends on what you would like to focus on. If there is an excess of *apas* in the relationship, simply imagine energy flowing from your heart to your partner's heart when you breathe out, and from your partner's heart to yours as you breathe in. If there is a lack of *apas,* imagine the same, but in the sacral chakra (3 fingertips below the navel, in the center of your body).

If there is an imbalance of sexual desires, then the one with a strong desire can imagine energy flowing from the sacral chakra to the partner's sacral when breathing out, and from the partner's heart to one's own on breathing in. The other person does the reverse, taking in the energy into the sacral when breathing in and breathing out the energy from the heart to the partner's.

Do this for about 10 minutes or longer if you feel the need to.

**Lifestyle**: Studies[5] conducted for over 70 years at Harvard show that the secret to happiness is in deep and fulfilling relationships. Unfortunately, this is a message that hasn't yet reached out to people and even when it has, it hasn't sunken deeply enough – because we have been programmed for too many years to believe that happiness lies in that brand new car, that brand new house, a bigger salary, a more beautiful face or partner, fame, success and what not. When we meet people, we automatically have more respect for the person who drives up in an expensive car, than for the one with a bigger heart and possibly, a bigger smile even. I know that even the idea itself that something other than money can bring people joy is unacceptable to some.

Happy relationships bring to life what in Ayurveda is called *rasa*. This roughly translates to 'juice', and it is the secret behind taste, vitality and vibrancy. When our *rasa* is depleted, our body dries up, we age faster, cannot enjoy the pleasures of life and feel dissatisfied. One of the easiest ways of physically restoring *rasa* is through regular oil massage. Heavy oils like mustard oil help greatly in winters, sesame oil when the weather is hot and dry, and coconut oil when the weather is hot and humid.

Emotionally, kindness, forgiveness, non-attachment, compassion and non-violence help in sustaining healthy *rasa* in the body. Practice patience and awareness, and step out of potential emotional dramas. Balance work with play, make sure you get enough time to engage in activities that nourish your soul.

Physically, dancing is one of the best ways of balancing the water element in the body. The more flowing the movements, the better it is – so hip-hop isn't exactly ideal for this purpose, but belly dance is great. Slow and flowing *vinyasa* yoga sequences, Tai Chi and Qi Gong can also help. Swimming in the pool and in the ocean are both deeply healing for the water element in the body.

**Work**: When *apas* is in balance, work can flow easily, moving around obstacles and finding solutions effortlessly. When out of balance, it can get slippery, with a tendency to take on more than can be handled, miscommunication with clients, stagnation and sluggishness.

Acknowledgement and awareness are key factors here. Work tends to push us into a mindless focus on accomplishing tasks. Learning to remain present while at the same time remaining focused on tasks can help to bring about a balance and better efficiency.

## Meditating on *Apas*

Imagine that you are on the surface, deep in the middle of the ocean. Now imagine yourself gently floating downwards, comfortably and able to breathe easily. Become aware of the temperature of the water, the wetness, and how it makes you feel. Allow yourself to go deep until the color of the ocean is a deep blue.

**If your body is dry and lean:**

Imagine your body absorbing the water, and the water coming in and healing, nourishing and soothing every cell in your body.

Remain in this state for about 10 minutes or longer. When you're ready, allow yourself to come to the surface of the ocean. Become aware of the light in the sky. When you are ready, slowly open your eyes.

**If you tend towards excess weight:**

Become aware of the water within your body, as well as the water outside. See carefully if the water within looks turbid.

Imagine the boundaries of your body disappearing, and feel yourself merging with the water. Let the healing waters come in, purify and cleanse your whole being. Allow yourself to dissolve until you are nothing but a light in a healing waters.

Remain in this state for about 10 minutes or longer. When you're ready, allow a firm and strong body to form again, vibrating with your breath. Once it is formed, allow yourself to come to the surface of the ocean. Become aware of the light in the sky. When you are ready, slowly open your eyes.

**Note 1**: If you experience fear at this point, simply stay here, playing on the edge of the fear – not trying to escape it and yet not pushing it.

**Note 2**: Unfortunately rampant body image issues have caused normal people to think of themselves as obese. This is in part due to the lack of respect we have for nourishment – and its subsequent impact on the body. The second exercise must only be done if you are medically overweight, not as an attempt to force an already thin body to lose further weight.

**Breathing exercise:** *Sitali Pranayama*: To increase *apas* in the body, especially if you feel too much heat, this cooling exercise will help you find balance. Sit comfortably with your spine erect. Stick out your tongue and curl it as if you were wrapping it around a straw, and breathe in (if this is not possible for you, try this instead - stretch your lips as if you are smiling, teeth together and tongue at the point where they join. Breathe in through your mouth with a hissing sound.) Relax your tongue and breathe out through the nose. Continue for 1-2 minutes.

This is a highly detoxifying practice which also balances the digestive fire. It is especially useful in summer, when the body is parched and suffering from excess heat and a lack of moisture. It soothes anxiety and improves concentration and clarity.

**To reduce *apas*:** Excess *apas* in the body leads to weight gain through improper digestion. To remedy this, breathe through your right nostril 21 times a few minutes before you eat.

**Note:** Do not overdo this thinking that breathing through the right nostril all day will help you lose weight faster, as it can create severe imbalance, nose bleeds etc.

# PRITHVI (EARTH)

*Nature does not hurry. Yet everything is accomplished.*
*~ Lao Tsu*

Even with the first 4 elements, forming something stable and sustainable is not possible. As water gets even denser, it forms the fifth and final of the great elements – earth. If water brings in cohesion, the earth takes it to a whole new level, bringing in solidity and stability.

Its predominant characteristics are cohesion and obstruction. The qualities of *prithvi* are cool, stable, heavy, dull, dry, rough, gross, dense, and hard. Its solidity provides supporting force.

The word 'earth' can also imply clay, waiting to be moulded into something spectacular at the hands of a skilled potter. The earth thus offers potential for creation and manifestation. The earth element does not imply planet earth, but represents the solidity in matter and structure in the universe.

*Prithvi* represents the seed energy – the dormant energy latent within matter, ready to sprout into life through the interference of other elements. While *ākāsh* represents expansive emptiness, *prithvi* represents contraction and a wholesome stillness that is directed inwards.

The sense associated with *prithvi* is smell. As it evolves from the previous four elements, it can be perceived through all the other senses – we can hear it, touch it, see it, taste it as well. The sense organ associated with this element is obviously the nose, which also happens to be the hardest of all our sense organs.

The organ of action associated with *prithvi* is the rectum, responsible for the elimination of solid waste from the body. The quality of the stools can reveal a lot about the earth element in the body.

The body maintains *prithvi* in balance when there is regular consumption and excretion. If the body releases too much of this element through diarrhoea, then the body loses strength, while if too less is released due to constipation, the body hardens – it remains strong for a short while but the body becomes toxic.

The chakra associated with this element is the *Muladhara*, the root chakra located at the base of the spine. Energetically this is where our 'seed' energy is stored, and spiritual awakening starts with the awakening of this chakra.

The season associated with *prithvi* is late winter, when water has turned solid and everything is dry, cold, dormant, resting and contracted. As spring arrives, water begins to flow and brings this earth back to life.

In the cycle of life and death, *prithvi* represents the gestational period in the womb, where the body is formed. The child itself is relatively dormant, but the structure is formed, with the earth element providing the support for proper growth and development. The earth element continues to facilitate the development of the child even after birth until the growth is complete. A lack of the earth element at any point during this phase will affect the growth of the child.

A person with *prithvi* in balance will be forgiving, grounded, stable and capable of following a steady routine. Responsibilities will get delivered easily and effortlessly and the person is capable of doing much more in a short time than others. Physically, it manifests as thick skin, strong finger nails, large muscles, and coarse, dense hair.

Just like the beauty and design of a building is wasted if the foundation is weak, lack of the earth element takes away the foundation from our lives, leaving everything we've built prone to destruction.

There are many dimensions of existence in the universe, but few offer the intensity and range of experiences that this element has to offer. It is not only the densest, but also the only element that can be experienced using all 5 senses. This is why even light-beings take birth on earth every once in a while, because it is the only place where experiences can be this deep.

One of the common misconceptions of human existence is that the sole purpose of human lives is to 'wake up'. How different is this from saying that the purpose of acting is to realise that one is not the role one is playing? You are the universe trying to experience what it is like to be you. Some of those experiences can only be possible if this memory is temporarily wiped out, just like actors sometimes experience a blurring of the boundaries between their own personalities and the personality of their role. Just as this is an ecstatic process for an actor, being human is an ecstatic experience for the soul, even if the 'role' itself seems negative or painful. When the time comes to experience human existence along with the awareness of our true reality, people start 'waking up'.

Because of its density, this element is considered a hindrance in some spiritual pathways like *Raja yoga*. However, it must be borne in mind that even in such pathways, the beginning is always based in a strong earth foundation through years of strict discipline under the guidance of a guru, intense *yoga asanas* and begging for alms.

Once the foundation is laid and the body is strong enough, the *yogi* begins by abandoning the earth element, giving up on food. Eventually water is given up, after which the need for warmth is sacrificed. It is at this stage one can come across sages walking in sub-zero temperatures wearing just a thin layer of clothing.

Over a period of time, breathing is also given up after which ether is given up, and the soul moves from the gross reality to the next level, that of consciousness. At this stage a doctor would find this yogi clinically dead, and India has known many sages who could move from being 'clinically dead' to life and back at will. Unfortunately, since these sages are famous for transcending the elements, people believe that abandoning the earth element is the spiritual way of life. This is not only untrue but dangerous.

When one tries to walk on any spiritual path without first establishing oneself in *prithvi*, it is akin to constructing a tall building without a foundation – it will eventually collapse, and this translates to physical and mental instability in a person.

# Imbalance: Causes and Consequences

A few decades ago, human beings had a much deeper connection with the earth. They worked in fields or did manual labor, they ate foods they had grown themselves, or that which was grown within a few miles away. Food was grown in nourished and healthy soil not drenched in toxic chemicals and were largely eaten fresh, not after remaining in cold storage. People lived in close knit circles and knew very little about far away people and customs. The earth element was very strong.

Now we live in a very expansive world. The earth element is very weak, with our bodies receiving very little real nourishment, our minds having very little stability, and our schedules becoming more unpredictable by the day. There is very little in our lives that supports the balance of the earth element in our bodies.

More and more we find people afraid of monotonous jobs, fixed schedules and commitment. Growth and expansion are expected all the time, without any scope for hibernation or recuperation. People reject the needs of the earth element within, and try to compensate by increasing the earth element outside – by filling their houses with things, their tables with too much food, or by taking up huge responsibilities that weigh them down.

Intense spiritual *sadhana* combined with fasting and renunciation also reduce the earth element.

The earth element relates to physical manifestation and practicality apart from rigidity and structure. So when the earth element is too strong, a person tends to become too rigid, remaining in an unchangeable routine for years and afraid of change. As this element also represents resistance, an excess can bring about a heavily pessimistic mindset, resisting anything new with resentment and suspicion. Greed and excessive attachment are also typical when *prithvi* is in excess, or if the person is trying to subconsciously compensate for a severe lack of the element.

Physically, excess *prithvi* manifests as excess fat in the body, but this differs from the fat caused due to excess water in that it is firm and does not vary easily. It causes a general feeling of heaviness, difficulty waking up, excessive napping, a heavy feeling after meals, etc. When too extreme, it can bring about excessive sleep, lethargy, or cysts/ cancer.

A deficiency of *prithvi* weakens a person and reduces the capacity to stand up for oneself, and the resilience to taken on the challenges presented by life. There is no capacity to structure one's life and stick to a routine, no matter how essential. There is fear of commitment, grounding and taking up responsibilities.

Deficiencies in the earth element in the body result in a weakness of body structures. Lacking in the raw materials to build solid tissues, the bones become weakened and osteoporosis places the bones at risk of fracture. Muscle mass is reduced and body fat decreases. As one function of the earth element is to retain heat, the body's ability to regulate internal temperature decreases and an individual easily feels cold. Lacking in substance, a person with a deficiency of earth is unable to stand up against the challenges of the world and is easily pushed aside by stronger forces.

## Balancing *Prithvi*

**Relationships**: This element can have a very stabilizing, grounding and nurturing effect on relationships when in a balance.

When out of balance, it can bring the relationship to an inert state, where people have simply resigned themselves to the lack of involvement in each other and just co-exist. If just one person has too much of it, it can lead to rigidity and a difficulty in accepting changes in the other, as well as in embracing the changing phases of the relationship. The other might feel 'weighed down' by a person who has an excess of the earth element.

A lack of the earth element can cause commitment issues, difficulty in settling together into a new situation, discontent in the relationship and a difficulty forgiving the other.

The earth tends to be static, so any kind of movement will shake things up. Going for a run together every morning or traveling together without a fixed plan can help couples rediscover their joy. To balance a deficit of this element, massaging each other's feet or meditating on the earth together can also bring healing and stability.

**Lifestyle**: When *prithvi* is balanced, a person is content, stable, reliable, efficient and unperturbed. An imbalance will make a person either rigid or frivolous.

Nothing heals an imbalance of this element more than direct interaction. Gardening is one of the best ways to balance the earth element. Science is catching up, and there are studies to support gardening as a therapeutic tool.[6] The beauty of connecting with the earth is that the earth grounds and balances – so there is no risk of the earth element going out of balance when we connect with the earth.

*Prithvi* slowly decreases in the body as we age, warranting a change in eating patterns and general lifestyle. The healthiest people are those who gradually start reducing the quantity of their food as they age, as this helps their system remain in sync with the change. Reducing activities like shouldering big responsibilities and letting the younger ones take charge, along with practicing gentle and compassionate detachment helps people integrate this change the most gracefully.

**Work**: The qualities that *prithvi* brings, like structure, support, reliability and stability are all critical to being successful at work. Too often now a days, we have people who conceptualise magical ideas but fail when it comes to implementation. Earth people see things through to the finish, and usually with grace, ease and efficiency.

When out of balance, one can have the tendency to move from job to job without ever settling down and 'letting the roots grow'. Settling down is almost seen now a days as a drawback, as something that prevents one from growth. But unless one can root oneself in one place, real growth is not possible because real nourishment is not received. Growth without grounding is possible, but it will be shallow and transient.

A lack of *prithvi* will also prevent a person from asserting their stand, no matter how correct, in a meeting or with superiors.

Too much *prithvi* will make a person too rigid and resistant to new and possibly more efficient ways of doing things. Resistance to the kind of work itself also creates a severe imbalance.

To balance the earth element at your work place, it is imperative that you focus only on the task at hand, unless of course, multi-tasking is the very nature of your work. If there is a tendency to feel bored with the mundane, learning to embrace mundane tasks and allowing oneself to accept that it is possible to be happy while doing mundane tasks too will be very healing and stabilizing.

## Meditating on *Prithvi*

Being the densest and the most stable of all elements, this is the last one to go out of balance. So when *prithvi* is out of balance, one needs to be very focused on healing this imbalance through all ways possible.

**If you have too much *prithvi*:**

If there is too much *prithvi*, one needs to see carefully if there is also too much *apas* as well. If there is too much *apas*, meditate on *agni, vāyu* and *ākāsh* as outlined earlier, to bring healing to the earth.

**If there is too little *prithvi*:**

Many sensitive people with too little earth are aware that they are 'never in the body'. If this resonates with you then the exercise is really simple – sit comfortably and energetically come back to your body, occupying all of your body and being completely in your body and your body alone. If the lack of the earth element in your body is really extreme, it can feel suffocating the first time you do this, but just stay on as long as you can, and then repeat after a few minutes.

We have all of eternity to explore other realms, but we only have a limited time to explore what it is like to be a 'human being'. And this experience of being human comes with its faults, imperfections, difficulties and sorrow along with the positive experiences. When we remain outside the body all the time, we are essentially wasting our time on earth because all these situations and emotions are passing us by unexperienced. This also causes repetitive patterns as life tries to force us to experience it more fully, and often causes accidents too because pain is one of the ways of coming back to the body, if only partially. So if you continue this exercise daily over the next few months, you will find your life far more colourful, and you will be able to take pain and pleasure comfortably and in your stride.

If the above exercise seems too strange to you, here's one that involves imagination which will help you bring this element in.

Sit comfortably with your spine erect or lie down on the floor. Imagine that you are sitting on the earth (if you are not) or become aware of the earth beneath you. One of the most powerful aspects of the earth is gravitation and all of our lives we are taught to resist it – standing is only possible because our whole body resists gravity. Feel this gravity in all its intensity, and don't resist as it pulls you towards itself. If you experience changes in posture, that is ok, let it happen.

Now imagine that you are a pile of soil. Observe whether you see yourself as a big heap, small heap, and whether this heap is dry or wet. Become aware of your breathing and imagine that you are breathing as this soil, coming to life. Let the earth you are on, connect with you and heal the imbalances in you.

When you are ready, slowly imagine that soil turning back into your body again, but deeply connected with the earth at all times. Gently open your eyes when you're ready

# POWERFUL COMBINATIONS

*Growth is never by mere chance.
It is a result of forces working together.*
~ *James Cash Penney*

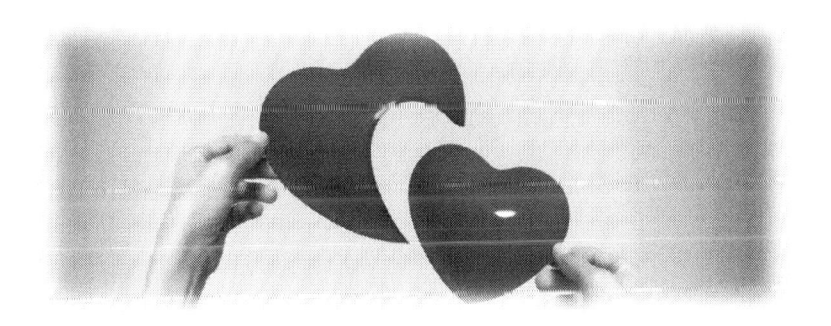

The elements come together to form a few powerful combinations which play a major role in our health: ether and air, fire and water, and water and earth. Ayurveda calls these *vata*, *pitta*, *kapha*. They perform the functions of destruction, sustenance and creation.

# *Vata*: Ether & Air

*Vata* is the combination of ether and air. Ether gives air the space to move around and manipulate life within the body. A lack of space will prevent the air from moving freely, and a lack of the air element itself will reduce the life force energy within the body.

In combination with ether, air manifests as five different kinds of *vāyu* in the body.

The most important of these is **prana vāyu**, also often considered life force energy itself. The seat of *prana* is the heart, where it resides in union with *ahamkara*, the ego[7]. Literally translating to 'forward moving air', it governs the movement of energy from head to the navel, which is the *pranic* centre in our physical body. It governs inhalation, the intake of sensory impressions and our receptivity to healthy sources of physical, mental, emotional and spiritual nourishment,

**Apana Vāyu** literally translates to 'air that moves away' and governs the movement of energy from the navel to the root chakra. The seat of the *apana vāyu* is the core of the pelvis and it is gives movement to the earth element in the body. It governs exhalation and release of carbon-di-oxide, elimination of wastes from the body, as well as the elimination of toxic thoughts and emotions. It protects us from false teachers as well as harmful energetic and astral influences.

*Udana Vāyu*, literally translating to 'upward moving air', governs the movement of energy from the navel up to the head. The seat of this *vāyu* is the throat and it regulates the ether element in the body. It is responsible for directing the utilisation of the energy created in the body. So it is responsible for directing the energy generated through exhalation including speech, and directs the energy generated during various bodily processes to the right organs. It governs joy, strength, enthusiasm, our spiritual growth. During sleep, *udana vāyu* moves the mind to dream and deep sleep states. After death, it is *udana vāyu* that is responsible for the movement of the soul from the physical to the astral and causal planes.

*Samana Vāyu* translates to 'balancing air' and governs the movement of energy from the entire body back to the navel. The seat of this *vāyu* is the navel and it gives movement to the fire element in the body. It governs the absorption of oxygen by the body during the retention of breath. It governs all kinds of digestion in the body, whether physical, mental, emotional or spiritual, and provides nourishment, contentment and balance in all these areas. It regulates our internal fire with adequate fuel. It is this force which enables us to remain centred and connected with our core.

*Vyana Vāyu* translates to 'outward moving air', governs the movement of energy from the navel outwards to the whole body. It pervades the whole body and gives movement to the water element in the body. It regulates the direction of circulation of nutrients to various parts of the body. It is responsible for the health and clarity of all the channels in the body through which *prana* flows. Mentally, it is responsible for a freely flowing mind. [8]

## *Pitta*: Fire & Water

Fire purifies and transmutes, and this is what ascertains the purity of our blood, absorption of nutrients and clarity of thought. However, fire by itself can be destructive, so these fires are balanced through the water element and together in Ayurveda they are referred to as *pitta*.

*Pitta* is a combination one might usually find intriguing. Fire and water are seen as forces that usually oppose each other. However, when they come together, they form acid – water that burns, an internal manifestation of burning hot lava. This is fire that flows downwards, facilitating digestion, absorption and assimilation. They are opposing forces nonetheless, and when out of balance can create a lot of problems. Too much fire will mean that it moves upwards instead of downwards, affecting digestion and drying up the body instead. Too much water and again, digestion will become impossible and the system becomes sluggish. Too little water, and the fire will not receive enough nourishment, fluctuating between becoming too sharp and hot, and becoming dull and ineffective, so in these cases you might find that both the too much fire and too less fire problems seem to apply.

The other two combinations are of similar properties, but this one is a mix of opposites. So a majority of the problems in the body is caused due to either the fire or the water going out of balance, and carefully studying and identifying the problem can help resolve it.

In combination with *apas, agni* works in five distinct ways in the human body:

**Pachaka Agni** is the fire that digests food and comprises of the stomach acids, the bile and other digestive juices.

**Ranjaka Agni** performs the secondary digestion and helps the nutrition reach the tissues. It fires up our circulation, purifying and energizing our blood, adding color and vigor to the body.

**Bhrajaka Agni** resides in the skin. It digests sunlight, oils ointments that the skin is exposed to, and converts it to the radiance of healthy skin. It maintains the temperature and complexion of the skin.

**Alochaka Agni** resides in the eyes. It digests visual perception and converts them into recognizable information. Spiritually, this fire helps us 'see' reality as it is, thereby assisting our growth.

**Sadhaka Agni** resides in the heart and is the seat of consciousness. It facilitates the brilliance that is a result of digesting information. It is responsible for intelligence and memory, and facilitates the digestion of ideas; this is what also brings the capacity to appreciate art and the finer things in life. It ignites the intellect and facilitates comprehension, sound judgment, discernment, transformation and ultimately, liberation.

## *Kapha*: Water & Earth

Water and earth combine to form deeply nourishing oil and phlegm in the body – called *kapha*. This combination lubricates and protects the body from drying, friction and consequent aging.

In the body, this combination manifests in the following ways.

**Bodhaka Kapha** is the salivary fluid and the mucous membranes protecting the lips, cheeks and the pharynx. It allows for the perception of taste and protects the mouth against the friction created by chewing and against the enzyme breaking down the carbohydrates in the mouth.

***Kledaka Kapha*** protects the stomach and the digestive tract from the acids digesting food. It lubricates and cools, also moistening hard foods to make them easier to digest. It assists in absorption and assimilation.

***Avalambaka Kapha*** is the mucous membrane that protects the bronchi and the lungs from drying up and also protects the pleura and pericardium from the wear and tear of continuous action.

***Sleshaka Kapha*** is the synovial fluid that moistens joint surfaces and resides in bursae, allowing tendons to glide freely over each other. It protects the joints in our body from continuous friction.

***Tarpaka Kapha*** is the cerebrospinal fluid that nourishes brain cells, stabilizes the flow of neurological impulses and protects nerves. It assists in the storing and recovery of all sensory experience. When it balance, it helps bring about contentment, peace and tranquillity.

# Doshas and Time of Day

According to Ayurveda, the doshas rule certain parts of day, and organs are more active at certain times and less effective at others. When we schedule our day to include these aspects, we can get more out of day.

Waking up before 6am is ideal, and anyone who has woken up at 4 or 5am knows how it is often much easier to wake up at this time, and there is a much stronger feeling of freshness. This is because this time of the day is ruled by *Vata* which rules activity and movement.

When we consider the ruling phases of the energies through the day, it is easy to infer that 4 to 6am is the time of the ether element. This makes it the perfect time to clear out the body as well as the mind. 4-6am is the time when the colon and bladder are the most active. This is also the best time of the day to meditate. Not only is this the 'ether' time for the body, but because this is the time most people are asleep and in the quietest phase of their slumber, this bringing down 'mental pollution' to the bare minimum thereby facilitating deeper meditation with minimum external interference.

6 to 8am is the time when the lungs are the most active, so this is the best time to practice yoga and some breathing exercises. Waking up at this time will increase *kapha* in the body, so it is not surprising that so many people need to shake off the heaviness by balancing it with a strong cup of coffee. Feeling heavy at this time of the day is an indication of imbalance and reducing dinner the previous night, having just fruits/ salads or skipping it altogether, along with of course waking up before 6, will be quite helpful. Emotionally this is a time when grief is the most predominant.

The pancreas get activated at 8am, so this is a good time for breakfast. However, it is still the *kapha* phase, so contrary to popular wisdom, a heavy breakfast or one with plenty of sugar is not advisable.

10am onwards is the time of the fire and water element, and productivity peaks. Digestion is the most powerful from 12-2pm, being the time of fire, and this is the best time for a nourishing, filling lunch. In addition, 2pm onwards *vata* kicks in, helping along the movement of the food. A time for air and then ether, 2 to 6pm is a good time for meetings and closing the day by winding up and clearing out the to-do list.

6pm *kapha* kicks in and starts slowing down the system. It is therefore best to conclude dinner before this phase begins. If one is asleep before the *pitta* phase begins at 10pm, the sleep will be much more nourishing and restful.

10 pm onwards is a time of internal activity, where your system is busy with cleansing. If you are awake in this period, you might find yourself reaching out for a midnight snack.

12-2am is the time when deep rooted and unresolved emotions are being brought to the surface, so postponing sleep beyond this time will prevent the processing of the baggage we have picked up during the day

The *vata* phase starts at 2am, so if one sleeps after 2, the mind will be restless and the sleep will be disturbed and the rest will not be deep.

Many artists and geniuses seem to wake up and function better during the night. This is because usually their *pitta* is weak. During the day, combined with the heat of the sun, the system gets too 'hot' to function with full efficiency, but combined with the coolness of the night, the heat of pitta brings about enough balance to fire up their engine and bring expression to their otherwise unexpressed air element. So if you are a night owl, working on your inner fire will not only remove sluggishness and make you more efficient during the day but will also solve your digestion issues.

# PUTTING IT ALL TOGETHER

*Dirt is matter out of place.*
*Weed is a plant out of place.*
*Nuisance is action out of place.*
*Even those things, acts or words which are normally good and useful become bad, useless, and even harmful when they are out of place, time and circumstance.*
*A knowledge of this fact is an essential part of wisdom.*
*~ Swami Krishnananda*

Earth is suspended in space. Water brings life to earth. Fire (warmth) brings life to water. Air gives life to fire. Ether gives freedom to air. Each element nourishes and supports the other.

The balance of the elements fluctuates under different conditions, and they can also transform into another element with the right treatment. For example, a candle which is predominantly earth element transforms into predominantly water element (melted wax) when lit and finally into fire and ether. As microorganisms break foods down either during the process of decomposition or digestion, primarily earth-based material transforms into ether (since the mass shrinks), air (gases released during the process), fire (energy), water and earth (the remaining mass).

If the conversion of something into ether is hard to conceptualise, here's a simple example. When we pour boiling water into a tight bottle and close the lid, we have poured predominantly the water and fire element. When we later try to open the lid, it is much harder because of the vacuum inside. Over time, the fire element has converted into ether and water.

## Time moves differently too

Science now agrees that time is a concept, is not linear and that everyone perceives it differently[9]. The balance of the elements also play a role in determining how time is perceived by a person. If this sounds bizarre, let us shift the perspective a bit. Think about it – when we are children, time seems to pass so slowly. One year seems like eternity. As we grow up, our world expands and a whole decade seems to have whizzed by in the flash of an eye. Expansion changes the perception of time.

So when the air and ether elements are in excess, time seems to fly – this also happens at mountain tops, where there is naturally more expansion and a greater element of air and ether. People with this imbalance are often late and feel like they've run out of time even though it only seemed like a few moments.

In contrast when the body is denser and the system more contracted, the perception of time is more expanded. So one can think of it as getting more seconds per minute. This allows such people to be highly efficient, be great at multitasking, and often have gigantic memories. They can also be fussy about being on time and hate being made to wait, because obviously – every minute seems like ten!

## The Microcosm and the Macrocosm

Everything can be viewed in terms of the five elements. The body of course, is formed with the five elements, but we can view all of existence from this perspective, including the elements in the periodic table and even the atom itself!

The earth element represents the mass of the electron, protons and neutrons, along with the sub atomic particles. The water element is responsible for the cohesion between the sub atomic particles. The fire element is responsible for the electric charge contained in the atom. The air element is responsible for the movement of the electrons. And the ether element represents the space within the atom. When the balance between the elements in an atom is tampered with, we get the atomic bomb, which unleashes the power of the fire element as the water element (which keeps the fire in check) within the structure is broken down.

The planetary system can be viewed from a similar perspective, as can each cell in our body. The earth element forms the structure of the cell and the plasma membrane, water element the water within the cell, fire element takes care of the metabolism in the mitochondria within the cells, the air element brings in the oxygen and space the vacuoles.

Similarly, food, parts of the body and living spaces can also be viewed in these terms, giving us a chance to bring about a balance by manipulating these aspects of our lives.

# Imbalance ≠ Negativity

When people tell me that they want to live completely positive lives, I often respond by saying that they should then stop using electricity, because that is purely the flow of electrons. When used correctly, this negative charge 'lights' up our lives quite literally!

Negativity is not really the problem. In terms of elements, outward, upward flowing elements like ether, air and fire are considered positive, and water and earth are considered negative as they create contraction and flow downwards. People with too much 'positive' energy effectively have too much of the first three elements, creating the imbalances already outlined in the previous chapters. A person with too much of the expansive elements will lose energy too fast and get tired easily. This may make them good psychics and healers but it will be at the expense of their own well-being. It is impossible to clear the system of waste matter without downward flowing energy. It also makes people too detached and incapable of deep emotions as well as empathy.

So, disease is not caused by 'negativity', as it is commonly perceived. Just like electricity 'lights up' our lives, correctly placed negative emotions can light up our lives too, anger helping us draw boundaries when needed, for instance, and fear helping us protect our lives.

As Swami Krishnananda so aptly puts it, that which is out of place, time and circumstance becomes harmful and potentially toxic. An understanding of this is critical, as problems can then be seen as an imbalance, and not negativity which needs to be removed.

## Five Elements in Life

When we start to study life in terms of the five elements, a lot of things start to fall into place. Take decision fatigue, for example. Having to make plenty of decisions is found to be more tiring than moderate physical activity and leaves a person trying to escape decision-making by either choosing the most obvious choice or trying to defer decision-making[10].

Decision-making is intense mental activity and increases the air element in the body. Air is an outward moving element and will lead to quick fatigue. The body tries to compensate either through avoiding further activity or by trying to increase the earth element – either through sleep or food – and this is substantiated by the studies, which find that people experiencing decision fatigue are most likely to reach for high carb-high sugar foods[11], which is exactly the sort of food that will increase the earth and water element in their body, bringing about a temporary balance.

It is interesting to also note how in places like India where there is an abundance of sunshine and often a dearth of rain, God is seen as a mother – some even consider the mother energy to be the foremost energy that existed before the Trinity came into being. People have an abundance of ether, air and fire, and crave water and earth – a nurturing energy which brings to mind the mother. In places where there is an abundance of rain and cold, people see God as the disciplining father figure – because they're craving for fire, air and ether. Of course, there are many parts of the world today where this isn't the case, and in these places there is an inherent imbalance that is creating destruction and chaos.

As human lives get more and more sedentary, people are trying to compensate for the lack of the air element through excessive thinking and traveling. People have never before travelled at this magnitude before!

As the space element increases through the lack of nourishing relationships, people seek to fill the void through food, and the body retains more to compensate. This is further accentuated with the already lacking earth element in our lives through the poor quality of foods and living in high-rise buildings.

This unconscious way of trying to compensate for the lack of one element is futile as it creates even more imbalance. When we make this process conscious, we can work towards balance instead of trying to blindly fill a void.

If you observe carefully what you are craving, that gives an indication of the imbalance in your body. If you are craving sweet things for instance, it indicates a lack of the water and earth element, which means that eating something nourishing and tissue-building – like proteins, would help your body reach a balance.

If you're craving for sweetness from relationships, it is an indication you are refusing to provide yourself a nourishing and stable mental and emotional space, and seeking to compensate this through others. Taking better care of yourself physically as well as mentally and emotionally and learning to draw clearer boundaries will help heal this.

The beauty of understanding life from the perspective of the five elements is that it allows us to bring about a balance in more ways than one. If a break-up is leaving a person feeling a big void in life, for example, one would understand why one is trying to compensate for the excess ether (sudden emptiness) through excess earth (food). Without this knowledge, one would be left grappling with relationship issues on the one hand and the emotional eating on the other, seeing them as completely separate issues instead of just one problem.

When we start to look at it from the five element perspective, it is easier to find a solution, and we can find healthier ways of bringing balance instead of resorting to subconscious unhealthy patterns.

# OTHER PHILOSOPHIES

*Everybody lives their lives differently.*
*They have a different perspective.*
*They've been through different things in love.*
*They've cried about different things.*
*~ Luis Fonsi*

Much of the world has also at some point or the other, viewed material existence from the perspective of four or five elements. The ideas have slightly varied, and the extents to which this knowledge was applied to various aspects of existence, has been diverse. In the West, this knowledge seems to have been more as a means of understanding the world and for alchemy, whereas in the East it seems to have been used extensively for healing as well.

One of the earliest Egyptian sacred books, Kore Kosmou (*Virgin of the World*) with Isis and Horus as the teacher and the taught, mentions the four elements, air, fire, water and earth. These texts are referred to as "Hermetic writings" by the Greek and attributed to the Egyptian God of wisdom, learning and literature, Thoth. [12] In 1909, Egyptologist Flinders Petrie suggested that the Kore Kosmou may be as old as 510 BCE.

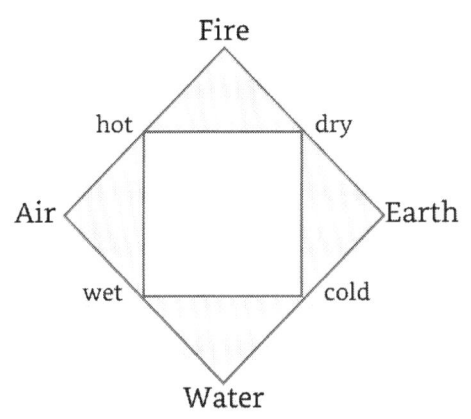

According to one of the most accomplished medical researchers of antiquity, Claudius Galenus, these elements were used by Hippocrates in describing the four humours in the human body: blood (air), yellow bile (fire), phlegm (water) and black bile (earth). [13]

Around 450 BC, Sicilian philosopher Empedocles suggested the four 'roots' – air, fire, earth and water. He also proposed attractive and repulsive forces he called Love and Strife which united and separated the elements.

Aristotle later related each of the elements with properties, hot, cold, wet and dry and also added a fifth element aether.

The Babylonian creation myth Enuma Elish written in 18th or 19th century BC, mentions the sky, wind, sea and earth as personified cosmic elements, although they are not considered to be the foundation of all material existence.[14]

Early Buddhist texts explained material world in terms of solidity, fluidity, temperature and mobility as a basis for understanding the root cause of suffering. Bön (Tibetan) and Godai (Japanese) philosophy both make use of the same five elements mentioned throughout this book and in Tibetan tradition were the foundation of many aspects of living, like medicine, astrology, psychology and spiritual traditions.

Chinese Wŭ Xíng is an extremely comprehensive system of interpreting the world in terms of the five elements. The five elements are wood, earth, water, fire and metal (wood similar in properties to the air element, and metal similar to ether).

The elements form two parallel cycles, that of creation and destruction. Water nourishes wood, wood feeds fire, fire creates ash (earth), earth gives birth to metal and metal holds water. In the same way, water douses fire, fire melts metal, metal chops wood, wood parts the earth (through roots), and earth absorbs water.

These principles have been used to understand and explain a wide plethora of subjects like tea ceremonies, traditional Chinese medicine, Feng Shui, astrology, cosmology, music, and even martial arts and military strategy.

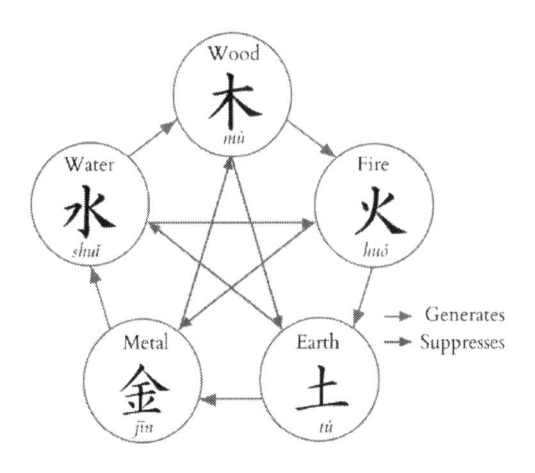

# FINDING BALANCE THROUGH FOOD

*Let food be thy medicine and medicine be thy food.*
*~ Hippocrates*

Food is one of the most essential aspects of healing when balancing the five elements. Various factors impact our body when we attempt healing through food. The taste itself, the impact of the related taste on our elements, the temperature at which it is served, whether it is fresh or processed, stale or coming from months in cold storage, the qualities it brings to the body, like stability, warmth, coolness etc, the vibration of the food itself based on the thoughts of the cook and the direction of its movement within the body all change the way food impacts our body.

Scientific studies often put all 7 billion human beings in the same basket when they study the relationship between foods and health, assuming that the results of a study on one location or ethnic group will duplicate across all other locations or body-types as well. Apart from this, foods are seldom studied taking into consideration weather patterns and seasons, an important factor in the efficiency of digestion and absorption.

# Ākāsh

Although ether actually has no taste, bitter foods have the highest ether element, and are hence considered the foods for ether. Bitter melons and gourds, fenugreek seeds, turmeric, leafy greens, barley, basil, nettle etc. are some examples of bitter foods. If a person is sluggish or lazy, these foods will help. Moist, heavy, satisfying foods also heal ether imbalance as they bring in the water and earth element and help balance the excess space.

Fasting once or twice a week also does tremendous good for the body, as several scientific studies[15] are starting to show.

# Vāyu

People with excess air have a tendency to eat very irregularly, especially since increased air in the body can create a tendency to either eat way too much or way too less – and this further disturbs the air element in the body and affect absorption. Especially if one is tending towards eating too less, there is a tendency to skip breakfasts, and this greatly aggravates the system. Regular balanced meals prepared using healthy (unrefined) oils and fats, served fresh and warm are very helpful. Ready-to-eat meals must be avoided as they lack *prana* – life force energy, contain plenty of chemicals instead and create disturbance in the body.

There has been a severe obsession with reducing weight and avoid fat for many decades, to the point that it has made many people sick. Healthy fats are essential to ensure that *vāyu* remains in balance and does not go out of control. Deep fried foods in small quantities are also nourishing if fried in healthy fats, and can bring about almost instantaneous relief in problems like constipation.

In general to balance the air element, favour warm over cold foods, oily and nourishing over dry foods, cooked over raw and slightly heavy – like grains, over light foods.

If suffering from an imbalance, it is a good idea to avoid caffeine, especially black coffee since it can make things worse.

# Agni

Healing the *agni* starts with healing the digestive fire, as this is also often the first to get affected. When the digestive fire is balanced, then absorption is good, there is minimal or no gas, and elimination is regular and healthy.

Digestive fire is strengthened through hot, spicy, sour and salty foods, so if a person has a weak *agni*, then these foods must be consumed in moderate quantities. Pickled and fermented foods, vinegar, yogurt, sour cream, cheese, buttermilk, sour fruits like unripe pineapples, papayas, grapefruits, peppers, beets, onion, garlic and spinach are some of the examples of foods that can increase the fire element in the body. Oils like almond and sesame, and spices like ginger and fenugreek are also helpful.

If there is too much *agni* in the body, the digestive fire needs to be pacified, and this can be done through sweet foods. Milk and butter help pacify the fire, as do sweet foods, with the exception of honey and molasses. Olive, coconut and sunflower oils, sweet fruits like grapes, melons, avocados, coconuts, pomegranates, mangoes, vegetables like cauliflower, beans, squash, lettuce, celery and spices like cardamom, fennel, coriander and cinnamon all help in soothing the fire.

How you drink water also affects the digestive fire. Drinking a glass of water a half to one hour before meals can kindle the digestive fire and prepare your stomach for a healthy digestion. Drinking water during meals, especially cold and sugary beverages reduce the digestive fire and impair digestion. A glass of warm water in the morning along with a teaspoon of lemon juice or apple cider vinegar and a teaspoon of honey also helps to balance the fire element in the body.

# Apas

Water is contained within and between the cells in our body and within blood vessels. The human body has a sophisticated system to manage the level of water in our body, and signals us through thirst when the body needs fluids.

Much of the water related problems caused in our bodies today is due to the fact that even the water we drink today is processed and not just devoid of life but also the wrong tonicity, which is the measure of water-electrolyte balance. Drinking water with too little tonicity (hypotonic) will deplete the body of essential salts, and if the tonicity of water is too high (hypertonic), it will dehydrate the body[16]. Most bottled beverages are out of balance, and most bottled water is hypotonic. Mountain streams and natural water are often the most balanced sources.

There are plenty of proponents of drinking a certain amount of water per day, but bodies vary widely in terms of size and natural tendency for water retention. More than drinking what others tell you, it is far more beneficial to learn to listen to the body and drink as much the body needs.

Water acts as detoxifying agent and plays an important role in helping with diseases caused by fire and air. For example, acidity, skin problems, constipation, dryness, excessive breakdown or accumulation of metabolites/endotoxins.

Keeping a bottle of water next to you and drinking whenever you feel like it usually helps to maintain a good balance. If dehydrated, it helps to get in essential salts and not just water, so combining water with oral rehydration salts or lemon, salt and sugar depending on what works for you, might be quite helpful in relieving the symptoms.

If you have water retention problems, drinking 2 glasses of water at a go is much more useful than drinking one or two sips at a time. Drink 2 glasses of warm water the moment you wake up, and about a half hour before every meal, and the last time an hour before you go to bed.

Foods that have a sweetish taste are abundant in *apas*, for e.g. cooked grains, non-fermented dairy, oils, nuts, and fatty meats.

Meats, or too much sweet, moist or oily food increases the *apas*, leading to a weakening of the digestive fire. As a result, the movement of food through the digestive system becomes slow and sluggish, the appetite is weaker and the abdomen feels heavy and bloated. These foods must only be consumed if the body is low on the water element, and that too in moderation, in small quantities at regular intervals.

A tablespoon of cold-pressed coconut oil mixed with coffee, milk or food can also help alleviate problems caused due to low *apas*.

# Prithvi

Food is a central theme with this element since it is through food that it enters the body. Since every physical manifestation is possible through the presence of the earth element, all foods contain some amount of it. The ones that contain the highest level of *prithvi* are grains, legumes, nuts and meats. When too much of the earth element is consumed, the excess is stored as fat. When too little is consumed, it results in reduced fat, but also weakened muscles and bones, the risk of osteoporosis and bone fractures, and the tendency to feel cold, since one of the functions of this element is also to retain heat.

# Tastes and the Elements

The five elements are also related to various tastes, and having a balanced meal regularly that includes all six tastes makes way for a balanced and healthy body. If cooking with the tastes in mind sounds too complicated, try just filling the plate up with various colours, or with various parts of a plant, for example root, bark, stem, leaves, flowers, fruits.

## Bitter: Air & Ether

Many people find this taste quite repulsive, but it has many health benefits.

The bitter taste scrapes the fat and toxins from the body and facilitates deep cleansing of the body. It kills germs, clears parasites from the GI tract, purifies the blood, clears congestion, and clears the liver while draining excess moisture from the body. It also reduces fainting tendencies and relieves skin problems like burning, itching and swelling. It enhances digestion, stoking the digestive fire and encouraging the release of digestive secretions and enzymes. [17]

Too much of bitter foods can weaken the kidneys and lungs and cause problems related to too much dryness like dry mouth, bone loss, reduced sperm count, confusion, dizziness and nausea. Bitter foods must be avoided if there is too much dryness in the body and should be minimized during pregnancy.

Some examples for bitter foods are leafy greens like kale and collards, eggplants, bitter melon, dark chocolate, coffee, sesame seeds and sesame oil, and spices like cumin, dill, fenugreek, saffron and turmeric.

## Pungent: Air & Fire

This taste is usually created by the presence of aromatic volatile oils, resins and mustard glycosides which stimulate the tissues in the mouth with a sensation of dry heat[18].

Its capacity to dry and warm makes it very useful in balancing excess water in the body. It flushes out mucous and toxins from the body, clearing the sinuses, dissolving clots and melting excess fat. It improves metabolism, circulation, increases sweating, purifies the blood, reduces cholesterol, heals itching and stimulates digestion, absorption and elimination. [17]

Air and fire both are drying by nature, so an excess of pungent taste in the food can dry out the mucous membranes in the body and kill sperm and ova, leading to sexual debility. It can also cause dizziness, fainting, burning, choking, skin problems, excessive bleeding, inflammation, diarrhea and colitis. [18]

Some examples of pungent foods are chilies, paprika, black and cayenne pepper, ginger, radishes, turnips, garlic, mustard seeds and greens, raw spinach, cardamom, cloves, buckwheat and spelt.

## Astringent: Air & Earth

The astringent taste is perceived as a dryness in the mouth, resulting from a contraction of the mucous membranes and creating a contracting, sometimes choking sensation. It is generally produced by tannins in the bark, leaves and outer rinds of fruits[18].

Together, air and earth lead to absorption of moisture, so this taste is helpful in stopping leakage of fluids, promoting clotting, cleansing mucous membranes, drying up fat, binding stool, etc. It can tighten loose tissues and help imbalances such as prolapses.

If consumed in excess, this taste can cause bloating, distention, dry mouth and throat, gripping sensation in the intestines, excessive thirst, excessive clotting, insomnia, and convulsions.

Some examples of astringent foods are fruits like apples, pomegranates, unripe bananas and cranberries, vegetables like alfalfa sprouts, avocado, broccoli, cabbage, carrots and most raw vegetables. Most beans are astringent. Wheat pasta and rye, and chicken and venison also fall into this category. Spices like coriander, caraway, basil, bay leaves, rosemary, oregano, parsley, poppy seeds, turmeric, vanilla and saffron are all astringent.

## Salty: Water & Fire

This taste is primarily present in the salt used in our diets.

It increases salivation, improves the perception of other tastes, stimulates digestion, absorption, assimilation and elimination, lubricates tissues, and helps maintain the water-electrolyte balance. External application of salt helps draw out moisture and reduces swelling and inflammation and speeds up the healing of wounds.

Salt is not only addictive, but it is also being used in excess quantities in processed foods and restaurants. This is dangerous for people who rarely cook for themselves. In excess, it can cause sodium and water retention, cause a thickening of blood, narrowing of blood vessels, increase thirst and blood pressure, cause ulcers, intestinal inflammation, hyperacidity, vomiting and infertility. It also aggravates skin problems and causes premature greying, baldness and wrinkles.

Examples for foods with salty taste are table salt, sea salt, rock salt, soy sauce, tamari, tuna, seaweed, cottage cheese and celery.

## Sour: Earth & Fire

Sour taste is the result of acid in our foods and it moistens and increases the flow of saliva in our mouth.

It helps with digestion, increases the absorption of minerals, activates the liver and stimulates the metabolism. It sharpens the mind and clears thinking. Most sour fruits are high in vitamin C, which is also considered to have antioxidant, rejuvenating and tonic properties.

If used in excess, sour foods can cause sensitivity in eyes, ears and teeth. It can cause fever, edema, wet cough, congestion, rashes, dermatitis, hyperacidity, heartburns, acne, eczema, psoriasis and blood related problems.

Examples of foods with this taste are sour fruits like lemon, lime, grapefruit, tamarind, tomatoes, dairy like butter, cheese, sour cream, yoghurt, alcohols, vinegar, and most fermented foods, including dough breads and pickles.

## Sweet: Earth & Water

The sweet taste brings to one's mind the taste associated with sugar, but that is not all there is to this. Sweet also includes the flavors of maltose and lactose apart from the common sucrose, fructose and glucose found in carbohydrates, proteins and fats.

Being the earth and water element, this taste nourishes the body, builds tissues and calms nerves. It rejuvenates the mucous membranes throughout the body, including the mouth, lungs, GI tract, urinary tract and the reproductive system. It improves hair and skin, speeds up healing of wounds, soothes burning sensations and makes the voice melodious. It improves longevity and strengthens, nourishes and energizes the system. It also soothes the mind and brings greater clarity and awareness in spiritual realms, which is why many religious places serve sweets to devotees.

The combination of earth and water elements – both inward-moving and attachment inducing by nature, make the sweet taste addictive. Too much can damage the digestive fire, destroy appetite, increase mucous, congestion, cough, breathing problems, and swelling in lymph glands. It can bring about fungal infections, worms, Candida, obesity and diabetes. It also makes a person excessively sleepy, lethargic and lazy.

Fruits like bananas, cantaloupes, melons, mangoes, dates and figs, vegetables like cucumbers, beets, sweet potatoes and cooked carrots, grains like corn, rice and wheat, milk, ghee, eggs, almonds, cashews, coconuts, salmon and heavy meats like beef and pork all fall under the 'sweet' category.

# MASSAGE & BODY SCRUBS

*Take the time today to love yourself. You deserve it.*
*~ Avina Celeste*

Massaging is a great way to balance the elements in the body. While oils are a predominant combination of water and earth elements, the way they interact with the body can balance a lack of the other elements as well. Regular massage is highly beneficial and can heal not only many physical ailments but also mental and emotional imbalances.

Those with a severe imbalance of the elements would benefit from daily massage. If the imbalance is not extreme, a weekly massage would suffice. Massaging during winters is especially beneficial since this is a very drying time and daily massage can provide anti-aging effect on the body. Massage during spring (or monsoons when closer to the equator) is ideal for removing toxins from the body and helping the body undo the damage of the past year, recover, repair and undo aging. A yearly intense massage ritual for a week accompanied with nourishing foods and plenty of rest can magnify these effects greatly.

## Benefits

Regular massage nourishes the body in many ways similar to the way watering a plant nourishes it. A warm bath helps the body assimilate the oil and absorb it effectively, helping the body benefit from the properties of the oil. It improves circulation in the body, slows aging, bestows good vision, improves skin and balances sleep patterns. It firms up muscles, and stimulates internal organs.

Massage normally implies application of oil on the whole body, but it could also be applied selectively. Application of oil on the scalp improves the quality and thickness of hair but it also soothes and invigorates all sense organs. The scalp contains nerve endings connecting to the rest of the body, so healing this part of the body is very beneficial. It also reduces wrinkles because massaging the head takes away the tension which causes facial muscles to tense up.

Applying oil to the ears can also be a good practice if the ear, neck or jaw have been problematic. It helps with infections and disorders in the ear and stiff neck and jaw. Sesame oil is a good option for application in the ear.

If you're too busy for regular massage, apply oil on your feet just before you go to bed and wear thick socks to protect your feet as well as the linen. This helps relieve fatigue and numbness of the feet, as well as rough skin problems. It also helps with vision and improves tissues, veins and ligaments linked to the feet. It is a very beneficial process for those suffering from excess of the ether element.

## Contraindications

While massage is deeply purifying and healing, it is critical to avoid it when there are too many toxins in the body or when the body is too weak. Here are the conditions where massage should be avoided unless recommended by a medical practitioner.

- Immediately after food, or immediately after taking emetics or purgatives.
- During the menstrual cycle
- During pregnancy
- If the tongue has a thick white coating on it, this is an indication of too much toxin in the body and massage should be avoided, or the toxins can spread to the rest of the body and be absorbed by organs and muscles.
- Over swelling, painful spots/ masses on the body, over infected or broken skin.

- During medical conditions or during acute illnesses like flu, fever, chills, food poisoning, indigestion.

Massaging is gentle and loving for the body and does not create any adverse effects. If you experience any discomfort after massage, it is important to visit an Ayurvedic/ medical practitioner.

## Process for Massage:

- Warm the oil (except in summers)
- Sit or stand in a warm room. Make sure there is no cold draft.
- Smear oil generously over your entire body.
- Massage the oil into your body, starting at the extremities and working your way towards the centre of the body. Use straight strokes on your limbs and circular strokes on your joints. Massage in large clockwise circular motion on the chest and abdomen. On the abdomen you follow the path of the large intestine, moving from the stomach to the left hip area, and from right hip area to the liver.
- Massage for 5-20 minutes lovingly and patiently. Brisk, hurried strokes increase the air element and will reduce the efficiency if you are doing this to nourish the body.
- Once a week, pay extra attention to the head, ears and feet.
    - For the head, start by applying the oil to the crown of your head and then work outwards in circular strokes.
    - For the ears, pour a couple of drops of the oil on a cotton bud or the tip of your little finger and apply this to the opening of your ear canal.
    - After massaging the soles of your feet, be careful to wash them off first to avoid slipping. Wear an old pair

of sock after bath to protect the floor from any residual oil.
- Have a warm shower or bath. If this is not possible, wear old clothes and go to bed, as the clothes will get quite soiled. Shower in the morning. It is best to use herbal powders to scrub the oil off instead of soap.
- Do not step into cold, windy areas immediately after the shower. If this is essential, make sure the body including the head and neck are well protected.

## Oils to Use

While the following information is aimed at massage, it can also be used with regard to consumption of these oils. Today most people use refined oils for cooking, and this is very unhealthy. Refined oils are oils with all the nutrition taken out, and often with added toxic chemical residues.

Cold-pressed or filtered oils are much healthier and should be chosen according to the weather and location. Oils pressed from plants that grow in the locality are the best choices. Using coconut oil when living in Manchester for example, is not the best idea since it is not local. Similarly living in India and using olive oil is not ideal. Companies benefit from selling their wares overseas, so imported oils are always hailed to be the next cure-all.

**Sesame Oil** is one of the best oils because it balances all elements. Despite being oily, it does not increase *kapha*. It heals imbalances of the ether and air element and even calms fire when used for massage. It goes into the deep-tissues, heals gas problems, helps gain healthy weight, improves strength and purifies the uterus. It can be used in all seasons and is especially useful in places where the weather fluctuates a lot.

**Ghee (Clarified Butter)** prepared from A2 milk also balances all elements and has many medicinal uses in Ayurveda. It is great for increasing vitality, longevity, intellect and strengthening the tissues. It also improves eye-sight and voice quality.

**Almond Oil** is a warming oil and heals imbalances of ether, air and fire but can increase the water element. It is very good for nourishing muscles, bones, plasma and the reproductive system. It is also good for the hair, skin, blood, memory and the brain. It must be avoided in cold and wet weather.

**Mustard Oil** increases fire, healing a whole range of problems caused by the coldness of the other elements. It also increases water and earth, which in combination with the fire bring about a deep nourishment and not the usual heaviness or dullness that is associated with them. It helps detoxify the body, strengthens the immune system, warms the body in winter and stimulates digestion, circulation and the excretory system.

The head and face must be kept cool, so applying this to these areas is not a good idea usually. However, if there is a sinus infection, applying it carefully on the face (it can create burning sensation in the eyes) and on top of the head brings great relief. If overdone, the eyes will feel hot and burning. This is also a very good oil to use in cold and dry weather. It also helps to repair the damage caused by too much or too little exercise. It must be avoided in hot weather since it can create too much heat.

**Groundnut/ Peanut Oil** is slightly less warming than mustard oil but more or less works in the same direction. It is very good for cold and dry weather. It can aggravate fire and burning in the body if the body already has too much fire or the weather is hot and dry.

**Coconut Oil** is touted to be the miracle cure recently. A decade ago it was demonised in India as everyone was told to switch to refined oils instead. It is essential to be careful about this kind of information.

Coconut oil is cooling, which is why it is most commonly used in places that are by nature hot and humid. Since the head must be kept cool, this is the ideal oil for the hair unless this is also how the weather is. Coconut oil is a little less effective when used in hot and dry weather, and must be avoided in cold and wet weather, because it can aggravate the water element in the body and cause an uncomfortable increase in mucous, cooling the body too much. It is wonderful for application on burning sensation, burns, sun burns, etc. and is helpful for skin diseases as well.

**Olive Oil** increases water and earth and reduces fire, air and ether. So it is not ideal for weight-loss. If used for massage, ideally it should be used during day time. It is wonderful with salads as it compensates for the high air element that raw foods bring to the body.

**Sunflower Oil** is a balancing oil and reduces fire and water. It is helpful with skin rashes, digestion problems, etc. It promotes healthy digestion, strengthens the nervous system, lowers cholesterol and neutralizes cancer-causing free radicals.

**Castor Oil** increases fire when consumed internally and decreases fire when applied externally. It is great for skin and hair, reducing wrinkles, acne, dark circles, inflammation and itching of skin, premature greying, and increasing the thickness of hair and eye lashes. It also helps heal dry skin and psoriasis.

**Linseed/ Flax Oil** increases fire and air. It helps reduce joint inflammation, arthritis, gout, back pain, heart disease, cholesterol and hypertension. It can aggravate skin diseases.

**Avocado Oil** is highly beneficial in treatment of excess ether and air. It helps with scaly skin, constipation, rough skin, stiff muscles, dry hair, joint pain, insomnia and improper blood circulation. It also helps heal imbalance of the fire element like ulcers, heartburns, poor metabolism and inflammation.

**Canola Oil** increases air and decreases all other elements, so it is good in hot and wet weather. Canola oil is extracted from genetically modified rapeseed and has not been tested for long term effects on health.

# Scrubs

Ideally one wouldn't use soap to wash off the oil. Soap may not be a bad idea if your drain has a tendency to get clogged up, but if that is not a problem, then using a homemade powder to wash off the oil helps improve the efficiency of the process even more.

A simple scrub that works for all skin types is chickpea flour or even better, horse gram flour. Adding turmeric and red sandalwood powder to this mix makes it more healing for the body.

Mix with yogurt if you have excess fire in your system and you can even rinse off with milk for added cooling. For oily skin, you can add fuller's earth to the mix and possibly powdered almonds, scrubbing the body vigorously. For dry skin, add honey and yogurt and wash off gently, following up with the application of a good moisturizer.

**Note**: Massaging regularly can mess your bathroom up. It is a good idea to give the floor a quick scrub with washing powder/ solution after each bath to prevent the accumulation of oils and eventual clogging. Towels will eventually get soiled too, so don't use new ones!

# MUDRAS AND THE ELEMENTS

*The mudra forms a vehicle for one's prana,
and helps both activate and exercise the prana one has.*
~ David Frawley

*Mudra* is a Sanskrit word which can be translated into 'gesture', 'seal' or 'attitude'. In the yoga tradition, *mudra* indicates a pose to direct bodily energies in a specific manner. Some poses involve the entire body, but to keep things simple, we just explore hand postures in this book.

Yogic philosophy correlates each finger to an element, and there are many *mudras* that are used to specifically direct the *prana* in one's body to achieve balance or spiritual growth.

These *mudras* can be practiced anywhere – in the bus, while reading a book, during a meeting, etc. However, doing them meditatively increases the benefit and takes the healing into the subtler layers of your body and mind.

For sick people who are unable to hold their fingers in a desired *mudra*, holding their fingers in position with rubber-bands also helps bring about benefits.

In general, there are three types of mudras[19].

**Tonifying Mudra**: When the tip of the thumb touches the base of any other finger, it has an effect of amplifying the element associated with that finger.

**Sedating Mudra**: When any finger is covered by the thumb, it tones down the impact of the element associated with that finger.

**Balancing Mudra**: When the tip of the thumb touches the tip of another finger, it balances the element associated with that finger with the other elements.

# Fingers and the Elements:

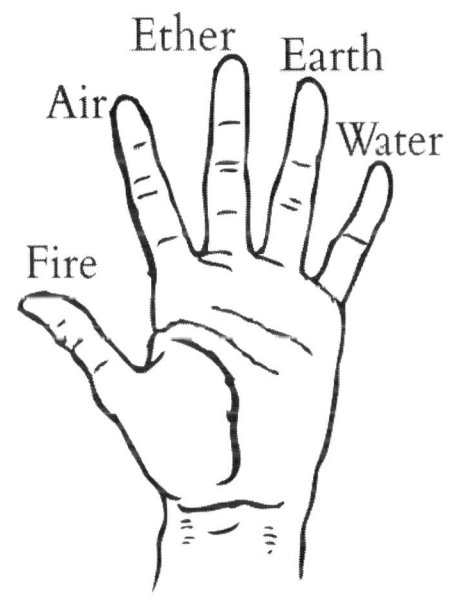

*Ether* — middle finger
*Earth* — ring finger
*Air* — index finger
*Water* — little finger
*Fire* — thumb

Thumb:          *Agni*    or   Fire
Index Finger:   *Vāyu*    or   Air
Middle Finger:  *Ākāsh*   or   Ether
Ring Finger:    *Prithvi* or   Earth
Little Finger:  *Apas*    or   Water

# The Process

Here are a few things to bear in mind as you practice the *mudra*.

- Do not practice right after a meal or during menses.
- Ensure your spine is erect, your lungs are relaxed and your breathing is easy and natural.

- Optionally, warm up your hands before you begin. Clap a few times firmly enough to cause a little stinging, then rub your palms vigorously.
- A gentle contact between the fingers is enough, there is no need to exert pressure. The remaining fingers might be held straight or be allowed to relax as per personal choice.
- Direct energy into your hands as you practice the *mudras*. If you practice energy healing, let the energy flow through your hands.
- Breathe deeply while you practice your mudra, and preferably practice with both your hands. If there is a constraint, you may practice with just one hand too.
- Be gentle with your hands, do not push it if it is painful. You may have a slight soreness after practicing initially, this is OK.
- For most *mudras,* it is ideal to practice 45 minutes a day, maybe in three parts of 15 minutes each, for optimal benefits. Some *mudras* can bring benefits within a few minutes too.

# *Ākāsh Mudra* (Increasing Ether)

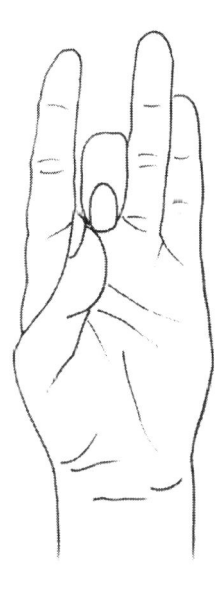

This mudra involves touching the tip of the middle finger with the tip of the thumb. It increases the space element in the body, enabling the individual consciousness to get more deeply in touch with universal consciousness.

It facilitates elimination of metabolic and toxic wastes from the body, heals high blood pressure and heart problems, relieves congestion and reduces the discomfort experienced after a heavy meal.

Practice it for 45 minutes daily (or 15 minutes three times), preferably around 2-6pm. Avoid this if you have a problem of excess ether.

# *Shoonya Mudra* (Decreasing Ether)

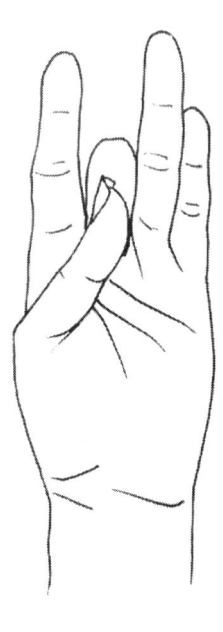

Pressing the middle finger down with the thumb suppresses the ether element. This heals problems caused by excess space in the body, like being accident prone, excess pain, tinnitus, vertigo, acquired deafness, numbness in the body, etc.

Since the element ether is associated with the ears, this is a very effective measure against any ear problem.

If this mudra is being practiced to reduce pain, preferably practice it continuously until the pain subsides. For chronic ailments, practicing 45 min ideally between 2-6pm as mentioned for the previous mudra is helpful. This mudra should not be overused, so stop using it the moment there is relief.

# *Gyān Mudra* (Increasing Air)

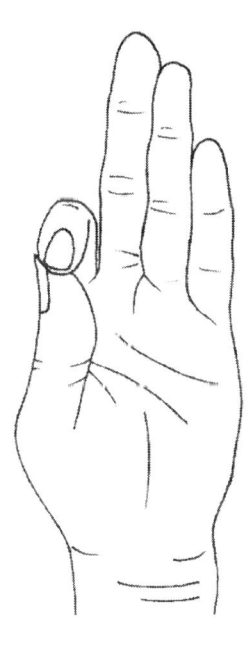

One of the most commonly used mudras in meditation, the *gyān mudra* is extremely beneficial, and is performed by joining the tip of the index finger with the tip of the thumb.

If this is practiced while meditating cross-legged, if the wrists rest on the knees and the tips of the three fingers point towards the ground, then this *mudra* brings detachment and a realization of the futility of material gains.

If the left wrist rests on the left knee and the right hand is placed in front of the heart with the palm facing outwards, it brings deep spiritual knowledge.

If the hands are raised to the side and held on each side of the head, it facilitates fearlessness.

If both the hands rest on each other in the lap, it facilitates rapid progress on the meditative path.

The increased air element in the body strengthens the nervous system, muscles, joints and cartilage, skin and mucous membranes, heart and pituitary gland. It calms and soothes the mind. It heals lethargy, drowsiness, loss of memory, and a wide variety of diseases related to the nerves and hormones, like Alzheimer's, MS, dementia, hypothyroidism, hypoparathyroidism, hypo adrenalism, hypogonadism, diabetes, myopathy, myasthenia gravis, paralysis, facial palsy, paraplegia, and the list goes on.

As with the previous two mudras, practicing this for 45 min between 2 and 6pm is ideal.

# *Vāyu Mudra* (Decreasing Air)

To practice this *mudra*, place the tip of the index finger on the base of the thumb and then exert gentle pressure on this finger with the thumb. This causes the fire element to suppress the air element in the body.

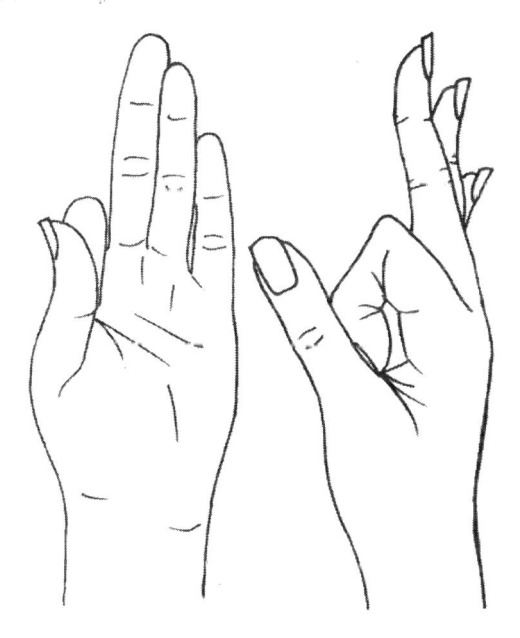

This interaction between fire and air soothes anxiety and calms the mind, nervous system, overactive nervous system and endochrine glands and facilitates the rehydration of the skin and articular cartilege. It relieves sleeplessness, epileptic fits, dizziness, hormonal imbalances, twitching, breathlessness, hiccups, consipation and dry/ brittle skin , hair and nails.

It is best practiced for 15 min daily between 2 and 6pm.

It needs to be stopped the moment there is relief, and must not be overdone.

# *Linga Mudra* (Increases Fire)

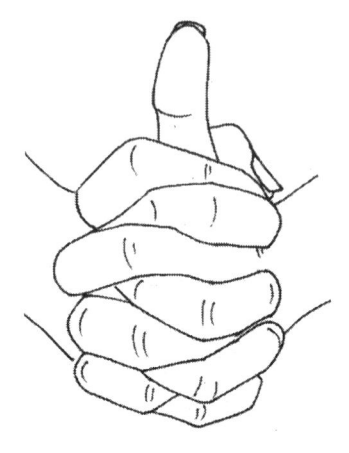

Clasp the hands, interlocking the fingers and holding the left thumb erect, for this *mudra*. Holding the thumb up reinforces the fire element and can help increase heat in the body in situations of shivering and chills due to inability to handle cold weather, excess phlegm problems like colds, sinusitis, asthma, etc.

This mudra should not generally be performed, and must be reserved for situations where the body is too cold, practicing until one is feeling better. It must definitely be avoided if there is fever.

# *Mushti Mudra* (Decreases Fire)

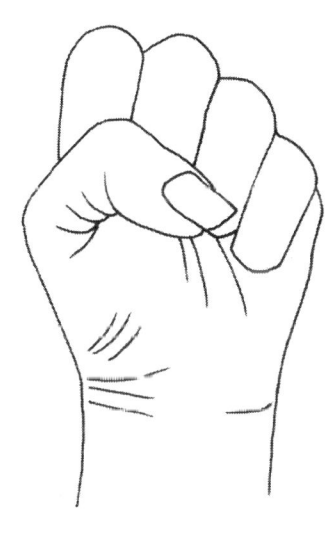

Make a fist with your fingers, placing the thumb on the outside. This *mudra* is great for digestion as it activates the stomach and the liver. It is also very helpful in releasing suppressed negative emotions, tension and worry, relieving constipation and lowering blood pressure.

Practice for 45 minutes as mentioned earlier, between 10am and 2pm.

# *Varun Mudra* (Increases Water)

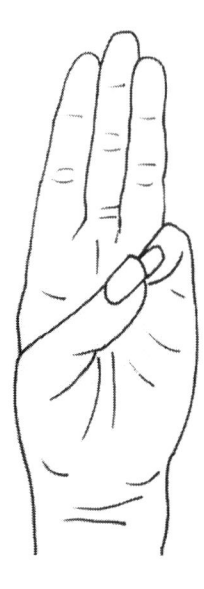

Joining the tips of the thumb and the little finger increases the water element in the body. Deficiency of water in the body is a cause for many ailments common today.

This *mudra* heals dehydration, dryness in eyes, skin and digestive tract, heals constipation, anaemia, loss of taste or tongue problems, deficiency of hormones, urine, semen and menses.

Practice for a total of 45 minutes any time of the day. People with excess water retention in the body should avoid this *mudra*.

# *Jal Shāmak Mudra* (Decreases Water)

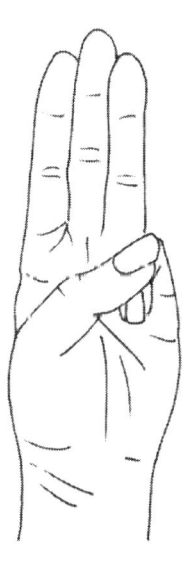

Bending the little finger to touch the base of the thumb and then pressing it with the thumb gently suppresses the water element with the fire. This leads to improvement in hyperacidity and diarrhoea. It decreases water retention, watering from the eyes, excess hormones and menses, and balances a cold body/ hands/ feet.

Practicing for 45 minutes as mentioned before is ideal, no specific time; it should be discontinued as soon as there is improvement.

# *Prithvi Mudra* (Increases Earth)

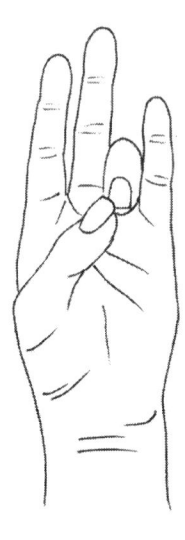

Joining the tips of the ring finger and the thumb increases the earth element and decreases the fire element. Since the earth element is related to the sense of smell, it helps disorders related to the nose.

It helps with lack of stamina, chronic fatigue, unexplained weight loss, fractures and bone, muscle and cartilage repair and paralysis. The strengthening of the earth element leads to increase in vitality, strength and stamina and a strengthening of bodily tissues like skin, hair, nails, muscles, tendons, internal organs, cartilage and bones. Since it reduces the fire element, it also helps with dry or burning skin, skin rashes, urticaria, ulcers, inflammation, hyperthyroidism, jaundice and fevers.

A total of 45 minutes a day between 6 to 10pm is ideal for daily practice. Those suffering from excessive lack of the earth element or excess of fire element can practice longer if needed. Those with excess earth element should avoid this *mudra*.

# *Surya Mudra* (Decreases Earth)

This *mudra* is performed by placing the tip of the ring finger at the base of the thumb and then gently pressing it with the thumb. This decreases the earth element and increases the fire element.

This is a wonderful *mudra* for people having an excess of earth element in the body. It helps heal very low body temperature, cold body/ hands/ feet, lack of sweating, shivering due to intolerance of cold, slow metabolism and poor functioning of the thyroid gland, obesity, weight gain, loss of appetite, indigestion and constipation. The increase in fire element means it heals eye problems as well.

This *mudra* is ideally practiced 45 minutes as mentioned, between 10am and 2pm or 10pm and 2am. Overdoing this mudra can cause over-heating of the body and consequent burning in the tissues and digestive problems.

# ELEMENTS AND LIVING SPACES

*He is happiest, be he king or peasant, who finds peace in his home.*
*~ Johann Wolfgang von Goethe*

Ancient Indian tradition combines architecture with the cardinal directions and the five elements. Balancing the energies in one's house based on the five elements helps solve many problems from the physical to the spiritual.

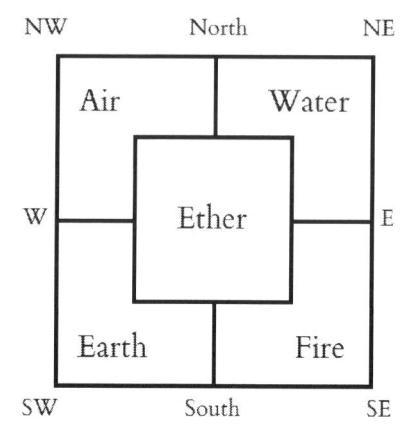

```
         NW         North          NE
         ┌──────────┬──────────┐
         │   Air    │   Water  │
         │     ┌────┴────┐     │
       W │     │  Ether  │     │ E
         │     └────┬────┘     │
         │  Earth   │   Fire   │
         └──────────┴──────────┘
         SW         South          SE
```

**Ether** rules the **central** portion of the house, and it is best if this space is airy, light and free. It is highly essential that this part of the house by completely free of any junk, or it can really 'weigh the family down'.

In general, plenty of space in a house facilitates clear thinking and creativity. One of the most creative artists I know lives in a nearly empty house with almost no furniture! Plenty of space also means (with the exception of space created as a result of poverty) that space utilization has been prioritized, so it helps the inhabitants be less distracted and more focused and clear with the priorities in their lives.

**Air** rules the **North-West** portion of the house and is a great place for windows, and anything that needs moving. If you do a home business selling things, this is the best corner of your house to keep your stock, it will keep moving! Obviously, not a great place to keep your safe or valuables as you would like these to remain. The owner of the house should avoid sleeping in this corner as it will lead to instability. This is, however, a good location for a guest-room or storing food grains.

The air element needs freedom of movement, so this corner also should be free from junk and clogging, or it may cause breathing difficulties in the members of the house and create problems in moving ahead in life. In general, having plenty of air circulation in the house facilitates joy, movement and freedom.

**Fire** rules the **South-East** corner of the house and is the best place for a kitchen or fireplace. Preferably, one faces South-East while cooking. If you find yourself facing in the opposite direction, placing a mirror in front of you so that you are effectively facing South-East, will help. Fire brings the capacity to put things into action, it brings power, drive, confidence and success.

Ensuring plenty of sunshine and a warm, healthy temperature in the house allows the fire element to be in balance. Exchanging the fire and the water corners in a house are usually responsible for the most problems in the household. Having a bedroom in this corner can lead to disturbed sleep and difficult relationships between the people who sleep in that bedroom.

**Water** rules the **North-East** part of the house, so obviously this is the best place to have a well, swimming pool, aquarium, fountain or a lotus pond. It is essential that the water in this space be alive and not stagnant, so if you have a stagnant water body in this location, place a few plants and fish in it to bring it to life. This is also a great spot to keep plants.

Water represents purification, cleansing and surrender, so this is also a great place to have your sacred space or altar.

Mirrors and glass also represent the water element, so having a large mirror in this part of the house also brings good energy. However, too many mirrors and glass furniture around the house can create an imbalance and result in depression. Water represents wealth too, so be careful to fix any leaking taps, they let wealth flow out and 'go down the drain'. Blocked pipes can block the flow of money into your house, and fixing these can unblock the flow and bring the money in.

**Earth** rules the **South-West** corner of the house and represents stability, firmness and being rooted. If this area is too empty or too open with many windows, it may leave the inhabitants of the house feeling detached and not grounded in the house. The earth also represents foundation, so having an underground water tank in this space can create problems. This part of the house is where the owner of the house should ideally reside, and is also a good spot to store heavy boxes. Of course, holding on to too much junk in this space leads to an excess of earth element.

In general, heavy furniture and furnishings represent the earth element. Covering the windows with heavy drapes reduces the air element (and also fire if they are always closed) and increases earth. Too much earth element in the house can create too much attachment to material and sensual pleasures.

## Cardinal Directions

**North**: The North combines the air and the water elements, bringing in the qualities of freedom of movement and prosperity. This makes it a good space for having the entrance or keeping money. However, sleeping with one's head in this direction can bring about nightmares and a disturbed sleep, as the energy finds it difficult to steady itself due to the air element, and the water brings up uncomfortable emotions.

**East**: The East is a combination of water and fire elements, making it a space of balance. Sleeping in this part of the house improves health when there are problems due to imbalance of these two elements, and also deepens the digestion of knowledge, so sleeping with the head in this direction is often recommended for students. It is also a great spot for generally spending the day, which means it makes for a good living space.

**South**: South is a combination of fire and earth, which bring in warmth and heaviness. Sleeping with one's head towards the South allows for a deep, restful sleep, providing the body the capacity to process and transmute the information of the day and also relax and rejuvenate the body. Obviously, this is a great direction for a bedroom.

**West**: The West combines the earth and air energies, bringing about movement as well as retention, so this is probably the best spot in the house to have a library or for children to study.

# ELEMENTS AND THE ZODIAC

*It's all about destiny.
That's why people look at the zodiac or the I Ching -
because there's a certain order to life,
and that order has been lived since the beginning of time.
No matter what you do, you're going to live inside of it.
~ Forest Whitaker*

Western Astrology considers four elements, skipping ether. Each element is associated with three Zodiac signs, and these signs exhibit certain similar characteristics.

It is important to understand that what is indicated through this information is not something that is fixed and definite, but an indication of the inherent tendencies within a person. With effort, a lot can be changed, including temperament, attitude and health. Those who are sensitive probably find it easy to understand the imbalance in their system. If it is unclear, studying the chart from this perspective helps us get a clearer understanding of what imbalances we need to work on.

One could simply look at the sun sign and draw conclusions about the elemental tendencies, but it is much more useful to have a look at the birth chart and see the distribution of planets. One doesn't have to know or understand much astrology for this, and free software online can help you with an astrological chart. One just has to observe the number of planet in each sign.

If the planets look fairly well distributed, then the person will have a balanced outlook towards life.

If the chart is heavily influenced by a particular element, the person will have a tendency towards imbalance, and will have to guard against an excess of that element in life through food, space and lifestyle.

Absence of a certain element in a chart means that the person will have a harder time connecting with this element and will have to bring about that element through effort so that balance can be maintained in life.

Having just one planet in one element will leave the person feeling like they are 'hanging by a thread' when faced with the issue of bringing the influence of that element into their life.

## Air Signs: Gemini, Libra, Aquarius

People with a lot of planets in air signs will have a strong influence of the air element, making them very social but in a detached sort of way. The air element is associated with the mind, intellect and logic, so these faculties are well developed. People having a strong air influence will have a difficult time fitting into a regular order of their surroundings. They need their freedom and space, emotionally as well as physically.

To work towards balance, a focus needs to be maintained on stronger water and earth elements and regular food timings.

## Fire Signs: Aries, Leo, Sagittarius

Like fire, people under the influence of a lot of fire are temperamental, dynamic, passionate, warm, outgoing and enthusiastic. The heat of the fire can make them quite dominating. When it becomes too much, they can be over-confident, pushy, aggressive, reckless or crude.

Water is obviously the most effective element to help balance fire. It brings in compassion, empathy and love. Something as simple as having a few aquariums in the right places can help.

## Water Signs: Cancer, Scorpio, Pisces

Unlike air which is logical and rational, water is emotional and gives importance to feelings. And unlike fire which initiates and self-promotes, water withdraws and protects itself. People with a strong influence of water signs are sensitive, psychic, compassionate and careful. When out of balance, this can make people fearful, suspicious, distrustful and too lost in their feelings.

Working with the air and the fire element will help uplift an out of balance water element.

# Earth Signs: Taurus, Virgo, Capricorn

A strong influence of the earth element makes people practical, matter-of-fact and grounded. They are loyal and stable, hard-working and know how to turn a plan into action. When out of balance, they can become materialistic, conservative, unimaginative and afraid of new things.

Working with the air element will help bring a disturbed earth element into balance.

## Qualities

|          | Air      | Fire        | Water   | Earth     |
|----------|----------|-------------|---------|-----------|
| Cardinal | Libra    | Aries       | Cancer  | Capricorn |
| Fixed    | Aquarius | Leo         | Scorpio | Taurus    |
| Mutable  | Gemini   | Sagittarius | Pisces  | Virgo     |

A study of the elements in the zodiac would be incomplete without also understanding the qualities of each sign, as these heavily influence how each element manifests in the sign. The zodiac can be separated into cardinal, fixed and mutable signs. As with the elements, studying the chart to see which one of the three dominates the chart will give a perspective into the personality.

A balanced chart will allow a person to work effectively internally as well as externally, being effective at starting, sustaining as well as taking a task to completion while being flexible around obstacles.

## Cardinal: Aries, Cancer, Libra, Capricorn

Cardinal signs are the ones which bring in a new season, so these are the initiators. They are great planners, creative and full of fresh approaches to solve a problem, but not always great at following up or seeing things through to the end.

## Fixed: Taurus, Leo, Scorpio, Aquarius

Fixed signs are those that exist in the middle of a season and are very driven, predictable and solid. They are not always good at getting the ball rolling, but once they have put something in motion, they are directed and focused, and answerable. On the other hand they may be rigid, and have a tough time handling unpredictable situations or changes in the original plans.

# Mutable: Gemini, Virgo, Sagittarius, Pisces

Mutable signs bring the season to a close. People who have a strong influence of mutable signs are very flexible, open-minded and adaptable. They can flow easily with situations and change their mind easily, although they can also often be indecisive. They can be all over the place, and when out of balance, can be unmotivated, too tolerant and unsteady.

# ESOTERIC TOOLS

*Do not wait; the time will never be 'just right'.*
*Start where you stand,*
*and work with whatever tools you may have at your command,*
*and better tools will be found as you go along.*
*~ George Herbert*

Several tools can be used to enhance the role of the elements in our lives. This knowledge is especially useful as a healer who works with people, as it becomes easier to heal imbalances you see in a client. While working on oneself though, it is essential that these tools are used to add to, and not to substitute the other important aspects of bringing about a balance, like changes in food habits, environment and lifestyle.

Exercise caution if you are trying the following without the help of an informed healer during sensitive times like pregnancy or serious illness.

## Essential Oils

Essential oils can be incorporated into our lifestyle by spreading the fragrance in the air using a diffuser or candles, adding them to your bath or applying them on the skin diluted in a carrier oil. One could even spray the curtains with it for a lasting fragrance. If you are making massage a regular part of your life, you could add a few drops to your massage oil for added effect.

**Ether**: The essential oil of Frankincense cleanses our energy, and Myrrh helps eliminate baggage which is holding us down, and Jasmine helps us connect with the divine. All these bring calm and tranquility, while assisting a spiritual practice.

**Air**: The essential oil of lavender helps release confusion and calm a busy mind. Lemongrass brings relief from aches and pains. They improve communication, intellect, eloquence, wisdom and facilitate travel, divination and freedom.

**Fire**: This element can be enhanced by using lime, orange, tangerine, clove, nutmeg. These facilitate better digestion, physical strength, communication, will power, purification and protection.

**Water**: Chamomile, eucalyptus, rosemary, spearmint, enhance the water element, promoting love, healing, peace, friendship, compassion, forgiveness, psychic abilities and cleansing.

**Earth**: Patchouli helps the body kick-start healing and repair. Sandal wood, cypress, vetiver and promote trust, peace and stability in the body, mind, relationships and finances.

# Crystals

Crystals have been used since ancient times for healing not just physical, mental and emotional problems but also external imbalances such as financial issues, relationship problems, etc.

It is essential to ensure regular cleansing of the crystals for them to work well and not intensify the problem. To cleanse a crystal, leave it in a bowl of water with a spoon of crystalline or rock salt for a few hours. Wash under running water and it is ready to be used. If you practice energy healing, you may charge it, or it can also be charged under the full moon.

## Selecting and Using a Crystal

When trying to work with crystals, the best approach is to let the crystal call out to you, instead of trying to use the head to select one. To do this, spend some time meditating on the element which you would like to balance, and request this element to reach out to you through a crystal. This may happen over the next few days or you could do this just before your visit to the store. If you feel drawn to a particular crystal, then it is right for you to use it. If you don't feel anything, it is probably not needed for your growth right now.

After you buy a crystal, cleanse and charge it before using it. Watch carefully for 24 hours when you use a new crystal – if it is not right for you, things tend to go wrong and if it is right, you can feel a positive difference during the day.

You could use a crystal as something to meditate with, or to place over your body as you heal yourself or clients, you could wear it as a pendant or a bracelet, or place it in your pocket or wallet to carry with you at all times. If you want to heal imbalances in your living space, you could place it in the right spot based on the element you want to enhance or reduce.

## Crystals and the Elements

**Ether**: Amethyst brings in the ether element and creates greater space within the energy field. Rainbow fluorite also helps in deepening one's connection to universal consciousness while at the same time grounding and harmonizing one's energy. Sugilite and clear quartz also help to dislodge unwanted negativity and clear the space, bringing about a healthy ether element.

**Air**: Rose quartz is a wonderful stone to set you free and help you drop old baggage. It purifies and opens up your heart and mind. Howlite is also a great stone for healing excess air problems. It reduces tension from mind and body and facilitates good sleep. Amber is great for healing problems caused by excess air, like fatigue, joint problems and anxiety.

**Fire**: Aventurine brings focus, heals anger and burnouts, and enhances leadership abilities. Carnelian brings motivation, inspiration and confidence, and kindles the fire in the right ways, burning away impurities. Citrine brings prosperity, tiger's eye strengthens the spine and sunstone brings in the energy of the sun to heal and balance one's energy field.

**Water**: Black obsidian is a good crystal for purifying the water element in one's body. The moon stone helps bring about balance. Selenite, named after the Greek Goddess of the moon Selena, helps to balance and stabilize the emotional body. Pearls, and aquamarine also deepen your connection to this element, bringing a balance in your emotional state and uplifting you.

**Earth**: Petrified wood is probably one of the best 'crystals' to bring in the earth element. It brings scope for new growth, provides energy to change one's path if needed, and helps ground oneself. Moss agate is another great stone for new beginnings. Black onyx helps improve grounding as well as get rid of unhealthy habits. Black tourmaline and yellow jasper are also useful, reducing the electromagnetic pollution caused by gadgets today.

# Devas and Angels

All religions agree that ultimately, everything is one. But just like one would need a plumber to fix a leaky tap, calling upon certain energies gives us access to specific help.

Christianity refers to these energies as angels, and four out of the seven mentioned in the Bible are in charge of the four elements (except ether).

Vedic and Buddhist culture personify and worship all aspects of nature and also pray specifically to the elements and have rituals to bring a deeper connection to these. In Vedic tradition, connecting with a planet is also a way of bringing in its qualities, so I also mention the related planet. One could meditate on the planet by visualising it or concentrating on the astrological symbol.

Any one of these could be prayed to or meditated upon for connecting with the transformative power of the elements. With

Hindu or Buddhist traditions, chanting related mantras also prepares your body for carrying that vibration more effectively.

**Ether:**

Goddess Saraswati governs knowledge and speech, and can help bring in divine knowledge that dispels any heaviness being brought about by the other elements. Gayatri devi also stills the mind, and the Gayatri mantra is a powerful way of tuning into spaciousness.

Ākashadhatvishvari or White Tara is the related Buddhist *Dakini*. She dispels ignorance and delusion and is the wife of Vairochana who represents consciousness and all-encompassing wisdom.

The Egyptian Goddess of the sky is Nut, Taranis in Celtic tradition and the planet related with this element is Jupiter.

**Air:**

Archangel Raphael represents the element of air and helps facilitate healing of the body, mind and spirit, releasing unhealthy blocks and burdens and setting you free.

Hanuman represents the power of the heart for healing and protection. He also helps *brahmacharya* – spiritual practice as well as in remaining celibate if that is being prayed for. He represents utmost surrender and being in service to the Divine.

Samaya (Green) Tara is the Buddhist *Dakini* related to the air element and eliminates jealousy and fear. She is the wife of Amoghasiddhi who represents formation and accomplishment.

The related Egyptian God is Shu, the Greek God of winds is Hermes, the Celtic one Borrum, and the planet which represents air is Saturn.

**Fire**:

Archangel Michael represents the fire element and burns away fear, making space for truth and courage. He helps you get closer to personal as well as spiritual truth.

The Hindu Goddess which brings in the qualities of Fire in a positive, gentle way is Lakshmi, the Goddess of abundance and prosperity. If there is a serious lack of the fire element affecting one's connection with inner power, it is beneficial to meditate on Rudra the fierce God who dispels sorrow and brings in peace.

The related Buddhist *Dakini* is Pandaravasini, the one who annihilates desire and lust, wife of Amitabha who rules perception and right discrimination.

The Egyptian God Ra is associated with the fire element. Ra was later merged with Horus. Meditating on the eye of Horus can help with inner power issues, although this must be done with extreme caution since it can easily create problems when out of balance. The related Greek and Celtic Gods are Hephaestus and Brigit, and the related planet is Mars

**Water**:

The Archangel related to water is Gabriel, who helps with understanding Divine guidance, and with learning spiritual lessons from our emotional and mental situations.

Goddess Ganga is one of the most powerful ways to connect with the healing power of water. Unlike normal water which goes stale and becomes undrinkable after a few days, the water of river Ganga remains pure even after months due to oxygen levels that are 25 times higher than normal water[20]. It was the only water the British used on their 3 month journey back to England because it stayed fresh, unlike the water they brought when they sailed from England which needed to be replenished[21]. Meditating on the Ganga brings purification, healing, nourishment, gentleness in temperament, peace and surrender. One could also meditate on the consort of Shiva, mother Gowri (known as Qwan Yin in the Buddhist tradition).

Buddhist *Dakini* Mamaki represents the water element and destroys pride and parsimony. She is the consort of Ratnasambhava who represents feeling and equality.

The Egyptian Goddess of water, moisture and fertility is Tefnut. The Greek God of the oceans, rivers, storms, floods, drought, earthquakes and horses is Poseidon. The Celtic Goddess of water is Ancamna, and the planet related to this element is Venus.

**Earth:**

Archangel Uriel is responsible for the earth element. He helps with grounding oneself in Divine knowledge and wisdom, along with bringing more stability in one's life and mind.

The elephant headed God of good luck, Ganesha, helps bring in the earth element and facilitates creation, financial stability and removal of obstacles. If there is a serious lack of the earth element, especially for women who find it impossible to 'stand their ground', it is helpful to pray to Goddess Kali who destroys that which no longer serves us, facilitates yogic transformation and the rise of the Kundalini.

The Buddhist *Dakini* related to earth is Locana, who dispels anger and hatred and is the consort of Akshobhya, who represents form and mirror-like wisdom.

The Egyptian God of earth is Geb, born of his father Shu (the god of air) and mother Tefnut (the goddess of moisture). The Greek Goddess Gaia, and Celtic Goddess Erecura represent the earth, and the planet associated with the earth element is Mercury.

# Tarot cards

The elements are well reflected in the tarot deck, with four elements being represented in the minor arcana, and the fifth in the major. These elements shape the energy of the suit and can indicate what your system is lacking, especially if a suit keeps coming up repeatedly.

One could even just pull out five cards to see if the elements are balanced. If there is one from each element, this is a clear sign of balance. If not, the imbalance will be well indicated, along with the direction in which one needs to work. One gets even more information if working with the negative cards as well. An inverse card from any suit would indicate the element being in excess or deficient, to the point of working against you.

**Ether** is represented by the Fool's journey or the major arcana, which is a representation of the journey of the soul.

**Air** is represented by the suit of Swords, which relates to the mind and the intellect.

**Fire** is represented by the suit of Wands, which are a call to action and relate to energy, enthusiasm, passion and vitality.

**Water** is represented by the suit of Cups, which relates to emotions, love, feelings, fantasy and imagination.

**Earth** is represented by the suit of Pentacles, which relates to the physical body, possessions, finances, work and manifestation.

## Music and Dance

Music and dance are great therapeutic tools and can help with balancing the elements as well. In general, the more primitive types of music and dance are more in tune with earth energy, and the soft, sophisticated ones are more etheric.

Symphonies, opera and church music which get us 'lost' and lose awareness of our body are all good to increase ether and air element. Such music without words or incomprehensible words increase ether and those with words increase the air element.

Music with lots of harsh and sharp sounds like rock and metal increase the fire element, and too much of these is dangerous for the system and can send it out of balance easily.

The water element is increased by music that touches us through emotions, even more so if it is music that is helping us release or get in touch with what we are feeling.

Listening to shamanic drums, Djembe or Tabla is a great way to increasing the earth element in the body. Indian classical music also has 'evening *ragas*' which increase the water and earth elements in the body, helping it to wind down for the night.

With dancing, the usage of feet can tell us a lot about the elements that are predominant in that dance. Ballet for example, is performed ideally on the tips of one's toes and increases the ether element.

Unless a dance is slow, almost all dances increase the air element, but probably ones focussed mainly on movement like the Indian style *Kathak* increases primarily the air element.

Dances performed on stilettoes like salsa, jive, etc increase the fire element. It is interesting how these dances often seem more like a display or power and passion than the display of affection and love. As the shoes have wider and stronger heels, like Flamenco and tap dancing play with the balance of fire and water elements. Flamenco also just happens to be a much more 'emotional' dance when viewed in the countryside.

Belly dancing takes it yet another step further and dispenses with the shoes, bringing in the earth element quite powerfully. The hip movement activates the water element, and this combination is quite powerful in releasing toxic emotions, healing depression and lethargy and healing from sexual trauma and blocks.

Dances performed bare feet and which involve stamping of the feet bring in the earth element very strongly. Many such dances also involve masks, bringing in the element of fantasy (ether and air) to compensate for the intense presence of the earthy movements. Some examples are the African *Kakilambe*, Vietnamese *múa lân* lion dance (which brings in the fire element as well, an earth, water and fire combine to ward off negative energies), and Indian *Bharatnatyam*, *Odissi* and *Kathakali*, to name a few.

# Including the 5 elements at your altar

Placing symbolic representation of the five elements at the altar can serve as a reminder if you are trying to incorporate this knowledge into your life, and also as a subconscious mode of bringing about healing and balance of the elements.

One easy way of doing this is by involving the five senses. This is one of the best ways to incorporate the five elements as involving all the five senses stills the mind the most effectively. One can see the use of it in several religious places of worship for the same reason.

A bell or music takes care of the ether element, joining the hands in prayer or holding a rosary takes care of the air element, a candle or lamp represents sight, or a photograph of a beloved God could also be used, a sweet, edible offering incorporates the water element and incense brings in the earth element.

Another way would be to represent the elements themselves. An empty vessel to represent ether, a flower, feather or incense to represent air, flame to represent fire, a bowl of water and a bowl of sand or ash to represent the earth.

Tibetan Buddhism uses mandalas representing all the five elements, which could also be placed at the altar. One could also use the elemental pentagram using Greek representations of the symbols as shown here.

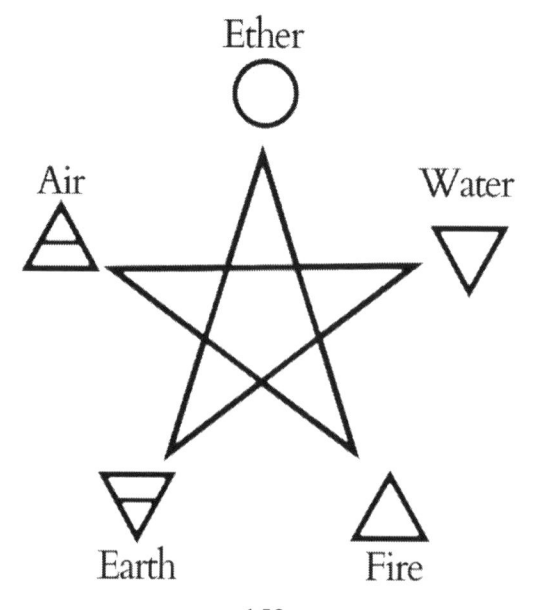

# THE IDEAL SPIRITUAL PATHWAY

*There are a thousand ways to kneel and kiss the ground;
There are a thousand ways to go home again*
~ *Rumi*

There are billions of people on the planet, and to imagine that there is only one path through which one can awaken to one's true nature is like thinking there is only one way to make a pizza.

There are thousands of paths, and it is completely possible that a very authentic and pure pathway transforming the life of a loved one may not be the right one for you at all. We have a tendency here to simply reject the other pathway as wrong when this happens, but this is a mistake. People are different, and different things suit different people.

Ancient Yogic texts classify spiritual pathways into four broad categories and these are easy to relate to the four gross elements on the basis of the temperament they bring about (Ether could relate to spontaneous awakening). There is a common misconception that yoga is exercise. In reality, yoga comes from the Sanskrit word *yuj*, meaning union. Yoga implies a journey which leads to the union of body, mind and spirit. There are instructions on how to proceed on each pathway in the yogic texts of course, but by no means do they claim to be the only path – ultimately the classifications listed here are about principle and not ideology.

## *Jnana Yoga*: The Pathway of Wisdom

Air personalities are analytical and rational, air being the ruler of the mind and mental activity. When in balance, the air element brings about clear thinking and foresight, and an ability to see both sides of the argument. For these people, the path of wisdom is ideal.

One uses the mind and experience to separate illusion from reality. As one moves forward, belief systems are dropped one by one through awareness and observation, and one reaches the point of renunciation of all desires, earthly as well as heavenly.

This path involves not only educating oneself on the theory through sacred scriptures and holy books, but also meditating on the information and integrating it. It includes studying actively the nature of one's own mind and self-inquiry.

The zen kōan (a question that provokes great doubt, for example 'What is the sound of one hand clapping?') and the path of 'Who Am I?' as taught by Ramana Maharishi is a good example for *jnana yoga*.

**The trap**: Every spiritual pathway has its trap, and this path also has a big one. People confuse this path to be the path of knowledge instead of the path of wisdom. Knowledge is of no use if it is limited to the understanding of the mind, and has not percolated into experience.

Wisdom makes a person humble, kind and loving. Merely knowledge expands the ego and makes a person more rigid, arrogant and makes them feel superior to others. In this path, people can easily get lost in the mind and this must be very carefully watched out for.

## *Raja Yoga*: The Pathway of Discipline

Fire brings passion, intensity, power and drive. When fire qualities dominate in a person, the pathway of willpower and discipline is ideal.

Raja Yoga is a path of intense discipline on all levels, physical, mental, emotional and spiritual. Gurus in ancient India would only take a person as a disciple on this pathway if he could sit still without moving for a whole three hours! Irrespective of where in the world this path is being followed, one usually starts with physical discipline, either through a strong physical practice, fasting, or both. One forces the mind to ignore the desires of the body, thereby creating detachment. It is easy to see why this pathway isn't for everyone.

Once the body is capable of remaining still for extended periods of time, the mind is then gradually trained to remain still through working with the breath and directing the thoughts in a specific way. Eventually one starts to enter thoughtless states, and this starts to burn away their impurities bit by bit, until they reach a state of complete realisation. This is the pathway of power, and brings with it many rewards along the way, many great psychic abilities, which is why this is also one of the most sought-after pathways.

What people think of as 'yoga' today is nothing but the third out of eight steps in this pathway of discipline (the first two being dos and don'ts). The ascetics meditating in the Himalayas for months without food, water and warm clothes are examples for *Raja yogis*, and they often have many supernatural powers as described in the many books written by people who have met Himalayan masters.

**The trap**: Many people on this path have sometimes gone too far and inflicted a great deal of suffering on their bodies, leading to early deaths sometimes, and big diseases in other situations. And then of course, there is a potential bloating of the ego when one can do a lot more than others in terms of physical and mental exertion. As this path brings psychic gifts, that is another big distraction, and people can get lost in them for decades, getting completely derailed from their pathway and becoming 'psychics' instead. It may be wonderful to have psychic abilities, but from the perspective of awakening itself, it is nothing but a major hindrance and distraction. As a Buddhist meditator once said to me – 'no matter what comes up, pay no heed', and this is a very powerful message to remember along this pathway.

# *Bhakti Yoga* – The Pathway of Devotion

Water people are empathetic, nurturing, loving, and greatly tuned in to their feelings. It would be obvious then, that love should be their pathway.

Our world is becoming increasingly intellectual and opinionated, and it is imagined that an ignorant person can get nowhere. I have seen this play out among people on the spiritual pathway too – one imagines that if a person knows very little, there is little scope of progress. But *bhakti yoga* defies this. One can make much faster progress on this pathway without any knowledge at all. True devotion is one of the fastest pathways to God.

That said, just like air and water have a very deep connection – air gives life to water, and water gives moisture and hence nourishment to air, *bhakti* and *jnana* often go together. Many people on the pathway of wisdom have been great devotees, and even completely ignorant people on the pathway of devotion suddenly have access to all spiritual knowledge once they awaken.

This path involves surrender and devotion, and may also involve music, dance, rituals and anything else required to celebrate the existence of their favourite God in their lives.

Many people and systems have been against idol worship, but an idol is often an integral part of this path as it provides the devotee something to relate to – it is much harder to feel love and devotion to a completely abstract idea.

Any religion or system that involves surrender to a particular God is an example for *bhakti yoga*.

**The trap**: *Bhakti* is the pathway of love, but it can very easily turn into the pathway of fear when people who are not right for this path try to walk it. One can revere, but one can never fear and love at the same time, so this can completely derail a person from their spiritual pathway. Then there can also be blind belief systems.

Then there is the 'my God is better than your God' trap, which is also so common. This pathway is about becoming so consumed in the object of one's devotion that one sees this object in everyone and everything – many have experienced this partially when they fall in love with a person. So when one is really on this pathway, there is no this God and that God, there is just one – ultimately the separation between the devotee and the Divine also disappears.

The last trap is that of inaction. People can have a tendency to become a pushover and let others hurt them in the name of surrender. One must see God in everyone, including oneself.

# *Karma Yoga*: The Pathway of Selfless Action

The earth element is closely linked to the material world and earth people are usually very responsible and dedicated. This makes it much easier for them to adopt the path of duty, or selfless action.

This pathway eradicates desire and the ego through doing what is 'right'. Irrespective of the way one feels about doing something, if it must be done, it must be done, and this annihilates the ego.

The path of *karma yoga* involves doing what needs to be done, while at the same time not being attached to the results or rewards for one's actions. It also involves being open to face difficult consequences for the right action if need be, like a soldier having to risk his own life and run through a line of fire to save the life of a comrade. 'Do your best, leave to God the rest' sums up this pathway very nicely.

It is hard to come up with an example for this pathway, but everyone we meet who may even seem to be an atheist or a non-believer, but is dedicated to performing his or her duty with utmost dedication is automatically on this pathway. These people are hard to idolize and often go unnoticed as 'spiritual' people because they usually seem very ordinary and rarely talk about spiritual concepts – they would rather focus on their duty.

**The trap**: The mind is a tricky thing and can lead to delusion. There are times the mind is convinced that an action is actually selfless where it is really guided by selfish motives. This needs to be guarded against, and a little help from *jnana yoga* (or a person walking that path) might be useful in this regard.

If one is following scriptures to determine what is right and wrong, it could be misinterpreted and lead to gravely wrongful action, again an area where inner wisdom could be of use. Ultimately, the heart knows what is right, and it is important to learn to balance theoretical understanding (or misunderstanding) with the guidance of the heart when it comes to right and wrong. *Karma yoga* without the guidance of the inner compass is a dangerous path.

Lastly, people on this path could fall into the trap of expecting others to also put duty above all else, and this could lead to a fair bit of misery and going astray from one's pathway.

# Ultimately...

These pathways are not mutually exclusive and do not conflict with each other. They all lead to the same goal, only that they need to be sincerely and rigorously practiced. [22] They complement each other, and one might find oneself practicing a little from all pathways at some points in time. However, in most cases one pathway will be predominant.

The guidance of an illumined teacher is of tremendous help in especially Raja Yoga and Jnana Yoga, but can also be of assistance in the other two paths, especially in helping avoid the traps. The search for such a teacher however, is quite pointless – when the student is truly ready, the teacher will arrive. Ultimately, sincerity and utmost honesty with oneself is the key.

# JOURNEYING THROUGH THE ELEMENTS

*The only journey is the one within.*
*~ Rainer Maria Rilke*

Manifestation of the elements makes its journey from the subtle – from the ether element to the gross – to the earth element. The spiritual pathway is about going beyond the gross realities of life and into the subtle aspects, so this journey takes the opposite direction.

This does not mean that one must try to reduce the heavier elements – indeed, one cannot travel far if the vehicle is damaged. This journey is not about eliminating or removing the heavier elements, but about transcending them one by one – and transcendence is not possible through rejection and suppression.

One's journey begins from the earth element, where one's survival is acknowledged and embraced. The first step is to learn to be in acceptance of the physical body, and to learn to be firmly established in it – too frequently we energetically abandon our bodies, especially if there has been early childhood trauma, and inner child work will help with this. You know your earth element is in balance if you find your energies 'resting' in your bottom when you are relaxed.

Once one is able to maximize the utility of the physical body and one's surroundings, it is time to accept and embrace the water element, the capacity to flow freely with life, and to enjoy emotions. Identifying, acknowledging and accepting one's emotions is the first step in this direction. Accepting one's emotions is not the same as acting them out however – so this is not an excuse to act crazy! Embracing and resting in one's emotions as a part of one's life experiences helps us transcend difficult emotions. We're frequently told to 'accept things as they are' and people tend to take this to mean we should accept the external environment – but it also means we need to learn to accept the internal environment.

It is only when one has embraced the body and the emotions that one can face, embrace and integrate one's true power.

Power in its raw form is extremely scary for most people, and this is why we see such an imbalance in the world – people are grabbing it from others or giving theirs away, seldom do we find a person resting in their own power. It takes a delicate balance of fire, water and earth to make sure this happens; water ensures fire doesn't go out of control and earth provides the substances which burns.

Once power games have been witnessed and transcended, one is capable of functioning without fear, and this creates the space for freedom and detached compassion, the air element. One has to pass through one's ideas of love, of giving and receiving affection and of trying to 'buy' love through various means – whether sacrificing oneself or being possessive – to be able to reach a state of balance, able to 'be' love. Without balanced earth, this love will never manifest as necessary action. Without balanced water, the love with never nourish. Without fire, it will be cold.

Freedom creates possibilities, and this brings about the 'space' for creative expression. In this part of the journey, one has to learn to transcend the desire to express without suppressing another's expression, learn to listen sincerely to others, the body and inner guidance, and be in acceptance of the limitations of one's own creative expression. 'The curse of an artist' is a popular term among those who create – an artist is rarely ever satisfied with a piece of work. Without earth, creative ideas remain in the mind and never turn into physical creation. Without water, the art remains shallow and misses depth. Without fire, the passion is missing, and without air, one cannot get into the creative 'flow'.

Eventually, the ego starts to take a backseat and the art just 'happens' – the 'artist' starts to disappear and magic starts to happen. At this point, one starts to transcend the material realm and move into deeper consciousness. One illusion after the other is acknowledged, witnessed and transcended, until none remain and one finally moves to the crown chakra – in union with the source.

The journey doesn't end here though. It comes back, bringing that oneness into the level of consciousness, into creativity, compassion, power, emotion and body so that one is able to participate in the world, and yet remain a mere witness.

# BIBLIOGRAPHY

*If you have knowledge, let others light their candles in it.*
*~ Margaret Fuller*

1. Laurence Hecht. "The Geometric Basis for the Periodicity of the Elements," *21st Century*, May-June 1988, p. 18.

2. Radin D1, Hayssen G, Emoto M, Kizu T. Double-blind test of the effects of distant intention on water crystal formation. *Explore (NY)*. 2006 Sep-Oct;2(5):408-11.

3.  Dorminey, Bruce, and Bruce Dorminey. 2017. "Without The Moon, Would There Be Life On Earth?". *Scientific American*.

4.  Asimov, I. 1973. *The Tragedy of the Moon*. New York: Doubleday

5.  Waldinger, Robert. "What Makes A Good Life? Lessons From The Longest Study On Happiness". 2015. *Ted Talks*.

6.  Soga, Masashi, Kevin J. Gaston, and Yuichi Yamaura. 2017. "Gardening Is Beneficial For Health: A Meta-Analysis". *Preventive Medicine Reports* 5: 92-99. doi:10.1016/j.pmedr.2016.11.007.

7.  Sivananda. 1997. *The Science of Pranayama*. Tehri-Garhwal: Divine Life Society.

8.  Frawley, David. 2006. *Ayurveda And The Mind*. Delhi: Motilal Banarsidass.

9.  Wolf, Fred Alan. 2012. *The Yoga Of Time Travel*. Wheaton, IL: Quest Books.

10. Anderson, Christopher J. 2003. "The Psychology Of Doing Nothing: Forms Of Decision Avoidance Result From Reason And Emotion.". *Psychological Bulletin* 129 (1): 139-166. doi:10.1037//0033-2909.129.1.139.

11. Tierney, John. August 21, 2011. "Do You Suffer From Decision Fatigue?". *New York Times Magazine*.

12. Brown, Brian, Nyhetep-Ptah., and Hermes. 2008. *The Wisdom Of The Egyptians*. [Charleston, SC]: BiblioBazaar. p. 178-200

13. Lindemann, Mary. 2010. *Medicine And Society In Early Modern Europe*. Cambridge [u.a.]: Cambridge Univ. Press. p. 19.

14. King, Leonard William. 2007. *Enuma Elish*. New York: Cosimoclassics.

15. Longo, Valter D., and Mark P. Mattson. 2014. "Fasting: Molecular Mechanisms And Clinical Applications". *Cell Metabolism* 19 (2): 181-192. doi:10.1016/j.cmet.2013.12.008.

16. Leiper, J. 1998. "Intestinal Water Absorption - Implications For The Formulation Of Rehydration Solutions". *International*

*Journal Of Sports Medicine* 19 (S 2): S129-S132. doi:10.1055/s-2007-971977.

17. Lad, Vasant. 2002. *Textbook of Ayurveda Vol I: Fundamental Principles of Ayurveda*. Albuquerque, N.M.: Ayurvedic Press.

18. Pole, Sebastian. 2006. *Ayurvedic Medicine: The Principles of Traditional Practice*. London: Churchill Livingston.

19. Carroll, Cain, Revital Carroll, and David Frawley. 2013. *Mudras Of India*. London [etc.]: Singing Dragon.

20. Hollick, Julian Crandall. 2017. "Mystery Factor Gives Ganges A Clean Reputation". *NPR.Org*. https://www.npr.org/templates/story/story.php?storyId=17134270.

21. Shukla, A. C, and Vandana Asthana. 1995. *Ganga, A Water Marvel*. New Delhi: Ashish Pub. House. p. 41

22. Adiswarananda. 2006. *The Four Yogas*. [New York]: Ramakrishna-Vivekananda Center of New York.

23. Gala, Dhiren. 2008. *Health At Your Fingertips*. Mumbai: Navneet Publications India Limited

24. Sharma, Shiv 2016. *Brilliance of Hinduism*. New Delhi: Diamond Pocket Books.

25. Bālakṛṣhṇa. 2013. *A Practical Approach To The Science Of Ayurveda*. Divya Prākāshan Divya Yog Mandir Trust.

26. "Ayurvedic Living". 2017. *Banyan Botanicals*.

27. Haplern, Marc. 2017. "The Five Elements In Ayurvedic Medicine". *Ayurveda College*.

28. Templeton, Kathryn. 2017. "About Vata". *Yoga International*.

29. Danielle. "The Ayurvedic Body Clock: Organs And Dosha Alignment With Time". 2017. *Svastha Ayurveda*.

30. "VPK Balance". 2017. *Maharishi Ayurveda Products*.

31. "Indian Scriptures". 2017.

32. "Chakras". 2017. *Cosmo Thai Yoga*.

33. "Astrology Zodiac Signs"

34. "Medical News Today"

35. "Pancha-Mahabhutas: The Five Subtle Constituents Of Matter". 2017. *Integral Yoga Of Sri Aurobindo & The Mother*.

36. "Pancha Mahabhutas The Five Sense Organs". 2017. *Ayurveda Medicine Treatment*.

37. "Five Elements of Nature to Attract Money, Growth & Success". 2017. *Astro Speak*.

38. "The Four Elements In Astrology". 2017. *Astrology Zodiac Signs*.

39. "Elements & Qualities". 2017. *Astrology Club*.

40. Research Center for Digital Humanities, NTU. 1995. *Digital Library and Museum of Buddhist Studies*. College of Liberal Arts, NTU. (Publication no. doi:10.6681/NTURCDH.DB_DLMBS/Collection).

# ABOUT THE AUTHOR

Ashwita Goel is a Reiki Master-Teacher, Hypnotherapist and Past Life Therapist based in Bangalore, India.

She is a second generation healer with over 20 years of experience in Reiki. Having learned meditation and Reiki as a child, she grew up to realise that she couldn't realign her priorities to suit corporate culture, and abandoned her career as a software engineer to teach Reiki professionally.

She works with individuals, groups and corporates, and has touched thousands of lives through Reiki and meditation workshops and personal healing sessions using Reiki and other energy healing modalities, EFT, hypnotherapy and past life therapy.

She can be reached through her websites www.reiki-bangalore.com, www.ashwita.com/zen, and her facebook page https://www.facebook.com/Reiki.Bangalore/

# ALSO BY ASHWITA GOEL

### Everything You Need to Know About Psychic Attacks
*Prevention, Symptoms, Solutions and More*

This book is a thorough guide on psychic and energy attacks. Ashwita Goel begins by guiding you through understanding psychic attacks, what makes you vulnerable, and how to separate the myths from reality. Then you learn how to identify whether someone is truly under psychic attack, and finally you are presented with solutions and methods of prevention.

### Healing Through Reiki

The same Universal Life Force Energy, which makes the buds bloom and the earth rotate, is within each one of us too. Practicing Reiki daily establishes that connection and empowers us. This book is meant for beginners, but also contains information that will be useful for experienced healers. It explains the concepts in a simple yet concise manner, and also covers the deeper aspects of healing.

### Reiki 101
*Answers for your Reiki Questions*

This book contains the top 101 questions asked by the Reiki Rays community, answered by five featured Reiki Masters.

Printed in Great Britain
by Amazon